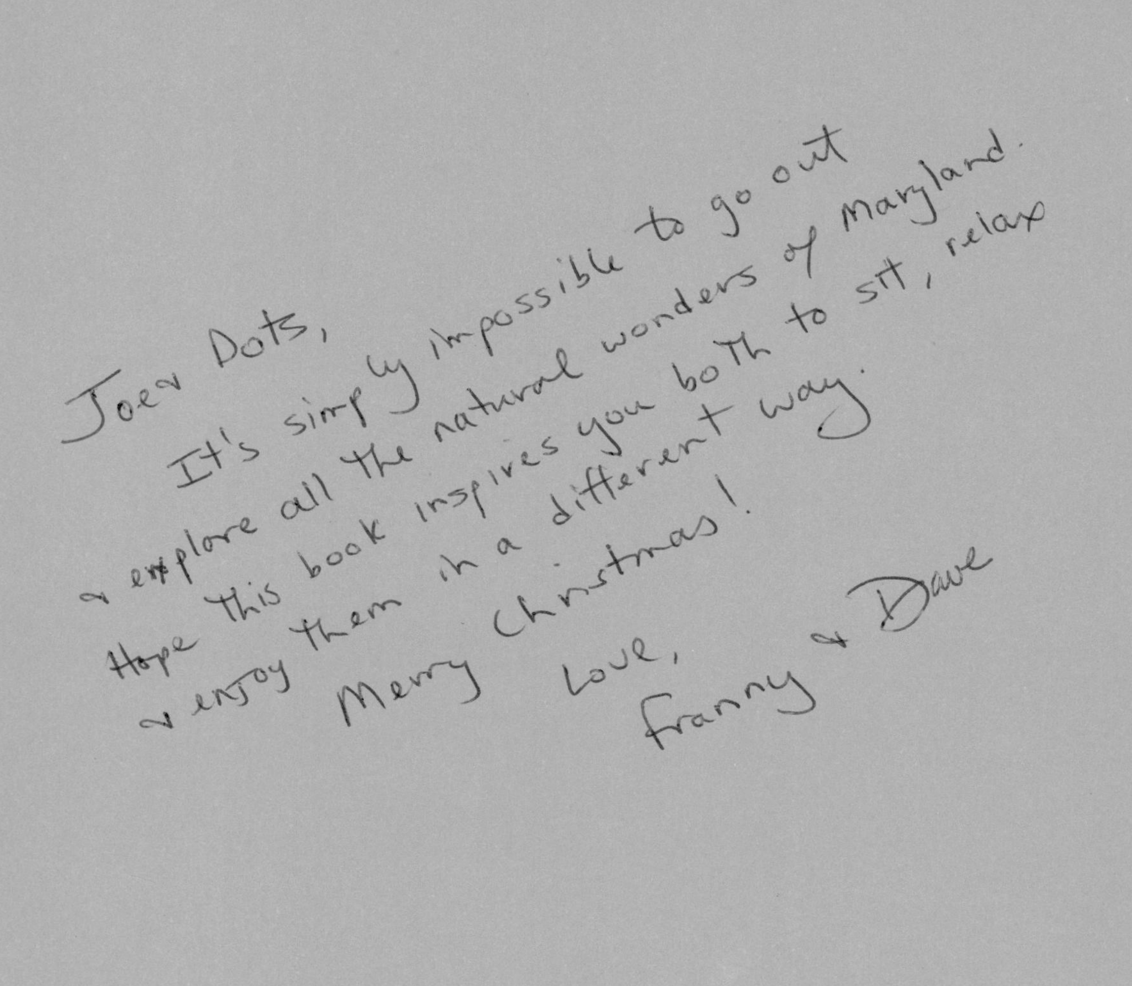
Joe & Dots,

It's simply impossible to go out & explore all the natural wonders of Maryland. Hope this book inspires you both to sit, relax & enjoy them in a different way.

Merry Christmas!

Love,

Franny & Dave

Middleton Evans

Maryland's Great Outdoors

Photography and Text by
Middleton Evans

Above: Showy Swamp Mallows and cardinal flowers frame a verdant landscape at McKee-Beshers Wildlife Management Area in Montgomery County.

Page 1: Set against a September dawn at Great Falls of the Potomac, a kayaker challenges nature's raw power.

Pages 2-3: Powerful and majestic, a rare northern goshawk mantles a vanquished ring-necked pheasant.

Pages 6-7: Crisp autumn winds draw kite enthusiasts to Ocean City's annual Sunfest Kite Festival.

Pages 8-9: Wearing his luxuriant fur coat, a red fox strikes a pose while traversing winter woodlands.

Pages 10-11: The North Branch of the Potomac River snakes its way across Maryland's ancient Appalachian Mountains in Garrett County.

Page 12: A massive 707-pound blue marlin is weighed in at the White Marlin Open—the world's largest billfish tournament, hosted in Ocean City.

Page 17: Lush summer greens of bald cypress trees and duckweed accent a freshwater marsh on Maryland's lower Eastern Shore.

Pages 18-19: Equally secretive and splendid, courting yellow-crowned night-herons share an affectionate moment at their nest on Smith Island.

Contents

International Standard Book Number: 0-9620806-4-0

Library of Congress Catalog Card Number: 96-94485

Printing and Binding: Toppan Printing Company • Singapore

Production Coordinator: Print Vision • Portland, Oregon

Typography and Composition: Baseline Graphics • Baltimore

Book Design and Text: Middleton Evans

Editor: Elizabeth A. Hughes

Publisher: Middleton Press, Inc.
7801 York Road - Suite 145 · Baltimore, Maryland 21204
Telephone: (410) 821-1090

TEAM

Introduction

Some days are better than others, as the saying goes, and once in a while a wonderful day takes you by complete surprise. Swinging back and forth in a hammock one summer afternoon at my parents' weekend retreat near Easton, I recounted some of my successes in recent months...splendid shooting stars in peak bloom, cryptic ghost crabs scurrying through my flashlight beam, and a close encounter with the "firebird," otherwise known as the scarlet tanager. O.K....so there was one shot—an oriole nest—from my lengthy springtime assignment list that eluded me, despite putting a dozen feelers out among my nature contacts. Who could be disappointed with a .975 batting average? Shaded by a grand old maple tree, I rediscovered the simple joy of tranquillity and a warm breeze. My well-deserved respite was complemented by music, in the form of chirping birds overhead. As the songsters turned up the volume, however, my curiosity got the best of me. I opened up my eyes to scan the branches for the source...and there it was, not twelve feet above, a neatly-woven basket, about the size of a baseball. I immediately recognized the handiwork of an oriole, and my weekend of R&R was over in the blink of an eye, as I sprinted across the lawn to retrieve my camera gear. Thus have been the past three years, a richly rewarding time of discovery, plenty of hard work, and a king's ransom of good fortune.

The seeds of my interest in nature were planted at a young age, but it wasn't until recently that they finally sprouted out of the ground. My early years were nurtured by a steady diet of nature programs on television—*National Geographic* specials, *Wild Kingdom*, hosted by Marlin Perkins, and scores of documentaries. Cuddly koala bears, roaring lions, and lumbering giant tortoises the size of beach balls came to life in our family room, my window on the natural world. Distinct childhood memories were also taken from nature, yet always far from Maryland...there were the prairie dogs from Wyoming, easily enticed into our motel room, one cracker, one inch at a time, and captured upon sliding the screen door shut; majestic bald eagles along Alaska's coast, the first I had ever seen, perched atop their conifer thrones; magical sand dollars beneath the surf of Georgia's Sea Island, so plentiful that my friend and I made a competition to see who could collect the most; a beautiful spotted stingray, flying slow-motion through the turquoise waters of St. Martin's, which I followed for half-an-hour before it disappeared into a reef; and fabulous waterbirds at the J.N. "Ding" Darling National Wildlife Refuge on Florida's Sanibel Island, so abundant, elegant, and unphased by the public eye, that it was the subject of my first and only professional wildlife photo adventure to date outside of Maryland.

Growing up in Baltimore, I cannot recall any poignant nature experiences other than our dog Sam barking at a family of terrified raccoons scampering up a tree. Camping, hiking and canoeing were not on the family agenda, and, with the exception of fun fishing trips on the bay, I was not aware that Maryland had wilderness areas. I could identify animals of the Galapagos Islands, Rocky Mountains, and the Serengeti Plains, but show me a ruddy turnstone, gray fox, or green treefrog, and I would show you a blank stare. No one ever bothered to tell me about native wildlife, and I never bothered to ask.

At the outset of my career in 1986, what I did know were all the things Maryland was famous for—horses leaping over four-foot wooden fences, watermen shaking blue crabs out of their pots, plebes at the U.S. Naval Academy scaling a greased-up Herndon Monument, boats of all shapes and sizes parading around the Inner Harbor, and an insatiable thirst for lacrosse— "the fastest game on foot." During the six years that I devoted to my first two books, *Maryland In Focus* and *Baltimore*, my assignments took me all over the state, but I rarely ventured into nature's domain, as I had little knowledge of our natural heritage, and therefore nothing to lure me in, or so I thought. All that changed in 1993, when I was ready to sink my teeth into a new project. To the best of my recollection, no one had published a pictorial record of our wild lands and creatures, from the marshes to the mountains. Perhaps it was time for someone to do so—and for me to rekindle that smoldering fire from the wonder years.

Like any diligent reporter, I first had to gather my facts, and thus set out to befriend a variety of seasoned naturalists who, much to my surprise, were eager to help. Their wealth of knowledge and encouragement would provide a vital lifeline to this project. I also scoured field guides, magazine articles, books, and television programs that highlighted our natural diversity. Perhaps 200 subjects were jotted down on a "wish list" that would both inspire and haunt me for the next thirty-eight months. The sheer variety of landscapes, plants, animals, and outdoor adventures that I encountered during a 50,000-mile odyssey would surpass my wildest dreams.

Though the line between fantasy and reality often narrowed beyond recognition these past three years, basic geology and geography would temper my bewilderment with logic. The structure and character of Maryland's land mass changes from region to region, and thus do the life forms that can be sustained. Consider this fact...a sufficient diversity of habitats are represented to entice roughly forty percent of North America's bird species; by contrast, the state's boundaries claim not even one percent of the continental United States. Another source of variance is our position along the mid-Atlantic seaboard. A number of typically northern and southern species reach the far limits of their range here, creating an unusual overlap. A perfect example is the bald cypress (pictured on page 17), a quintessential symbol of the South, though our trees are not draped with Spanish moss. Easily recognized by the knobby "knees" which poke up around its trunk, the bald cypress can be found along the Pocomoke River drainage in Wicomico and Worcester counties and along a narrow stretch of Battle Creek in Calvert County. Similarly, a common animal of New England and the northern tier of states is the porcupine, whose population is healthy as far south as Pennsylvania, but quickly thins out along the Maryland Line. Only a couple of documented sightings have been reported in recent years, but I was fortunate enough to photograph one vagabond porcupine that found its way to Harford County in 1994.

In telling the story of Maryland's natural heritage, human impact on the environment cannot be overlooked or overstated. There is much to admire today largely because nature is so dynamic and resilient, but the land on which the English settlers of the 1600s set foot was a far different place. Colonial Maryland was a heavily wooded, pristine natural community teeming with plant and animal life that is hardly imaginable by today's standards. Old-growth forests were abundant in hardwoods such as oak, hickory, and chestnut to the east and conifers like spruce, hemlock, and pine to the west. Coralroot and dragon's mouth orchids added a splash of color to wetlands and woodlands, also home to awe-inspiring carnivores like the cougar and gray wolf. Feisty fishers (a large weasel-like animal), pine martens, and perhaps some Canada lynx prowled through sprawls of red spruce in Garrett County, where snowshoe hares could never let their guard down. Bison and elk roamed a prairie that once stretched across the Hagerstown Valley. Overhead, flocks of passenger pigeons passed by, sometimes so thick that they could turn a blue sky gray. Dazzling Carolina parakeets, wearing green, yellow, and red, feasted on the seeds harbored in vast cypress swamps on the coastal plain. Wetland bogs, marshes, and swamps were far more common than they are today. The waters of the Chesapeake Bay were often clear to the bottom, where submerged gardens of aquatic grasses swayed in the changing tides. Clouds of fish shimmered by, as did a prehistoric-looking fish, the Atlantic sturgeon, armored with bony plates; it could reach lengths of fourteen feet. Yet sailors could not afford to admire the scenery for too long, as enormous oyster bars created navigational hazards that splintered many a bow.

During the next three centuries of settlement, Maryland's character was dramatically transformed. All but 1,000 acres of old-growth forest (Maryland covers some six million acres) would be logged to fuel a burgeoning economy. Glamorous animals, now only associated with the American West, like the elk, mountain lion, wolf, and bison were hunted into local extinction. Even common woodland animals like deer, turkey, beaver, and bear were harvested so heavily that only remote sections of western Maryland could offer sanctuary. Runoff from the agricultural and industrial landscape, including excess sediment, nitrogen, and pollutants choked the finely-tuned Chesapeake ecosystem, a problem yet to be solved. Dams on rivers prevented fish from reaching ancestral spawning grounds. Many of the bay's natural resources, once thought to be inexhaustible, have been depleted or otherwise imperiled to near oblivion by the hand of man. Consider the

oyster, a filter feeder which inadvertently cleanses the estuary's lifeblood. The present oyster stock requires a year to sift the entire volume of the Chesapeake Bay; traveling back two centuries, not even a dot on the evolutionary timeline, this mollusk was so abundant that it could do the job in a week. Wetlands were drained and filled in the name of progress. As recently as the 1960s, the agricultural pesticide DDT threatened the survival of bald eagles, ospreys, peregrine falcons, and other birds. On an even larger scale, hundreds of exotic plants and animals have been brought into Maryland for various purposes and since escaped to the wild, causing incalculable grief for native species. A prime example is the European starling; in the late 1800s some 100 "imports" from England were released in New York by one Shakespearian zealot (William penned a few words about these blackbirds), and millions of their descendants now fly over all of America, frequently evicting bluebirds, woodpeckers, martins, and other cavity-nesting birds from their nest chambers. The plant world has been hit the hardest, with perhaps as many as a fifth of today's species of foreign origin.

Enough of the bad news. As the conservation movement has shifted into high gear, the remainder of Maryland's wild lands, flora and fauna are being studied, protected, and appreciated as never before. Many of the forests have grown back, covering approximately forty percent of the state currently (though mature forests are not the same as old growth), and the vast majority of plants and animals that were living harmoniously before the plunder began are still around—some prospering as never before, others only barely hanging on. Exceptional parcels of wild lands representing many different types of habitat are still being identified and protected from development. The media is paying much more attention to environmental issues, and stories of honey-crazed bears, wayward manatees, and soaring bald eagles sway our emotions. Armed with more information, citizens are rallying in support of conservationists, who have posted many success stories in recent years, including the rebound of bluebirds, wood ducks, rockfish, beaver, and the Delmarva fox squirrel. Many species still face a precarious future, but the days of reckless harvesting of natural resources seem to be numbered, at least in this part of the world. I offer this book not as a mournful tribute to all that has been lost, but instead as a hopeful celebration of all that remains to admire and save in our natural world.

To my good fortune, I was able to work with a number of enthusiastic naturalists, including field biologists, animal rehabilitaters, botanists, watermen, fishermen, adventure seekers, conservationists, and weekend nature buffs, and through their generosity I am able to open this window to Maryland's great outdoors. Many of the subjects that appear in this collection are well off the beaten path, and not likely to be encountered. Luck was on my side the past three years, no doubt, and I paid my dues for a number of the more challenging subjects, but I never would have been able to witness such an array of natural treasures without the help of experts, who kindly shared guarded information. Many thanks to those who extended me their confidence and a helping hand....

A few words on my photographic techniques are in order. All of the original photographs reproduced in this book are 35mm transparencies, shot with Nikon camera bodies and ten lenses, ranging in focal length from 17mm to 600mm. The landscapes and wildflowers were recorded on Fujichrome Velvia; the wildlife and action images were shot on Fujichrome Provia. One of the biggest issues in the profession of nature photography is the use of captive animals. I acknowledge that a number of the wildlife images in this book were made under controlled conditions, either of animals in confinement or animals captured for the purposes of photography or scientific research and subsequently released. Some of the reptiles, amphibians, mammals, and raptors were photographed in this manner. The basic problem facing wildlife photographers is that most vertebrates, including many from this book, are instinctively distrustful of people, and their large "fear circle" keeps the onlooker at bay. Long telephoto lenses are only part of the solution; tricks of the trade must also be employed in many instances to bring difficult subjects into camera range. Captive animals can be a convenient shortcut around this arduous process, though they are not necessarily easy to work with. This is a good time to point out that the Maryland Department of Natural Resources has very specific guidelines as to what species may be collected or harvested from the wild; almost

all others are protected by law. Further, no form of non-game wildlife or native plant may be removed from public lands. The penalties for doing so are not insignificant.

From time to time a wonderful photo opportunity was presented by the powers that be and I failed to capitalize. Because I have no photographs to present, I will take this moment to describe these images that live only in my mind. First and foremost, hikers on the Billy Goat Trail in Montgomery County informed me of a colorful snake just up the trail, which I quickly found and identified—a handsome eastern hognose snake coiled on a sunlit rock. Face-to-face with the serpent, its reaction was as predictable as tomorrow's sunrise; first it flattened its head like a cobra and hissed at me, and when this bluff did not send me running, it rolled over and played dead, regurgitating its last meal—a wide-eyed toad which leaped out of the gaping mouth and hopped off into the woods. On another occasion, I was photographing a kingfisher perched on a favorite branch overlooking its nest tunnel. He was grappling with a minnow sandwiched in his bill, when, suddenly, a flaming Baltimore oriole appeared, landing just inches away to scold the trespasser. I pressed the shutter release on my motor drive, only to realize in a state of panic that I had already taken my last frame on the roll. By the time I had changed film, the birds had reached a truce and the oriole was on his way. I've also had a white marlin jumping in front of me, just as I have always hoped, only to be unable to target him during the second or two that the fish was airborne. Next time (if there is a next time) I'll not use a telephoto lens and simply crop in on the acrobat when printing. Speaking of watersports, I recall three racing log canoes approaching a mark, heeled over just in front of our chase boat. I finished my roll and was quickly reloading for the turn, when a sudden gust of wind capsized one of the boats, and the crew plopped into the bay from their precarious perches on the springboards. That's one shot I've always wanted, and I came so close.... I'm one of the lucky few Marylanders to have seen a wild coyote here, as it ran across a field near Aberdeen, but the instant we pulled over and made eye contact, at a distance of nearly 200 yards, it disappeared into the woods. Another time, a pair of equally rare "common" ravens, perched artfully in a dead tree, foiled my picture at the last possible moment by darting off with a laugh. Fortunately, the raven pictured on page 13 was not so snippety. This concludes my list of near-misses.

If the plants, animals, and landscapes that I was able to successfully capture on film spark an interest in nature, then I can offer a few suggestions. Concerning specific places to visit, two books recently published by the Johns Hopkins University Press are very helpful. *Finding Wildflowers in the Washington-Baltimore Area* by Cristol Fleming, Marion Blois Lobstein and Barbara Tufty, describes scores of natural areas in central Maryland and lists wildflowers commonly found in each location. The information is detailed enough that finding all but the rarest of local wildflowers should be relatively easy. Just remember, do not pick any wildflowers, and watch where you step. The second book, *Hiking, Cycling and Canoeing in Maryland: A Family Guide,* authored by Bryan MacKay, outlines a lifetime of possible adventures, with interesting vignettes about some of the specific species and habitats likely to be encountered along these trails. Many other books have been written about one or more aspects of the state's natural diversity, highlighting everything from a 2,000-acre botanical gem called Soldiers Delight (in Baltimore County) to the sixty-one species of butterfly that occur naturally on the Delmarva peninsula. They are all worth a good look.

If a yearning to volunteer is awakened, then many local conservation organizations and nature centers welcome assistance. The list includes the Maryland/DC Chapter of The Nature Conservancy, Chesapeake Audubon Society, Maryland Native Plant Society, Maryland Save Our Streams, Tree-Mendous Maryland, Maryland Ornithological Society, Chesapeake Bay Foundation, and Oregon Ridge Nature Center, to name a few. The Department of Natural Resources, based in Annapolis, has more information on these types of groups. Another simple way to make a difference is by contributing to the Chesapeake Bay and Endangered Species Fund on state income tax returns. Monies raised directly assist the DNR's mission to study and preserve rare plants and animals, as well as to improve the health of the bay. One final tip—if an injured or orphaned mammal or bird is encountered, there is a statewide network called Wild Bird Rescue to help collect and care for that animal.

Enough said by this novice naturalist. Let the pictures tell the rest of the story. Perhaps you will also be inspired to lace up your hiking boots and take a walk on the wild side. As for me, I'm returning to the hammock and finish my nap.

Middleton Evans
May 15, 1996

I Dedicate This Photograph To-

Dave Brinker

Brent Trautman

Dick Wiegand

Bob Rinker

Gerda Deterer

Robert Colona

Scott Smith

Tom Dembeck

Dee Thompson

Nick Spero

Kevin Dodge

Joe 0ndek

Joan Maloof

- for three years of shared expertise, encouragement, and assistance in the field.

The Land

Through the seasons and across the terrain, Maryland's landscape displays a remarkable variety of forms, colors, and moods. Considering that the mid-Atlantic region is arguably the least celebrated of America's vast mosaic of natural wonders, one might expect a preponderance of lackluster vistas. Yet the state's 10,460 square miles tell a story not of uniformity, but of contrasts, easily summed up in the familiar Maryland slogan—"America in Miniature." A quick look at geology explains the anomaly. The character of any environment is the sum total of several key variables, including soil, temperature, elevation, moisture, exposure, and contour. In Maryland, many combinations of these limiting factors are represented, yielding an assortment of habitats and plant and animal species that find refuge. Politicians have carved the state into twenty-three counties, but from the standpoint of a naturalist, it has five parts, physiographic zones called "provinces." All of the Eastern Shore and most of southern Maryland comprise the coastal plain, known for its flat topography, sandy soils, and smooth, slow-flowing rivers and creeks. Just to the west of the bay lies the Piedmont of central Maryland, where gentle, rolling hills are laced with streams babbling over smooth pebbles and ancient boulders. From Frederick County west, the traveler encounters larger obstacles, Maryland's mountains, divided into three distinct provinces—the Blue Ridge, Ridge and Valley, and Appalachian Plateau. Fundamental differences in underlying bedrock, elevation, and topography delineate each region. Let's not forget our most cherished natural resource, the Chesapeake Bay, a truly magnificent web of life touted as the world's most productive estuary. Though man has altered much of the environment, there are still hundreds of pockets of wild lands scattered throughout the state, where nearly 470 species of woody plants and 2,250 species of herbaceous plants can be identified. Highlighted on this extensive list are hundreds of flowering plants, a number of which rank high among North America's most spectacular wildflowers, including the swamp pink, American lotus, and yellow-fringed orchid. From mid-March through early November, this floral extravaganza unfolds across the landscape, leaving wildflower buffs just four months to catch their breaths for next season's rainbow of pastels.

Viewed at a distance, peatland bogs (above) *make a barren landscape, yet, upon closer scrutiny, fascinating details come to life. Bogs occur when wet depressions and ponds are colonized by sphagnum mosses, sedges, and shrubs, which form a floating mat of vegetation. Decaying organic matter settles to the bottom, compressed over time into thick, fibrous layers called "peat." Organic acids are released by the decay process, making bogs inherently acidic and nutrient-poor. Only highly specialized plants can tolerate these stressful conditions, including the insectivorous round-leaved sundew* (left) *and northern pitcher plant* (below). *While sundews ensnare flying insects with sticky droplets, the pitcher plant's urn-shaped leaves harbor fluid in which insects can drown.*

Previous pages: *A contrast of the seasons… Freshly-draped rhododendrons and pines overhang Tolliver Falls at Swallow Falls State Park in western Maryland. Fragrant pouches of a yellow lady's slipper orchid are a most inviting playpen for pollinating insects.*

Rocky areas form very specialized habitats that support a limited variety of plant life, such as this prickly pear **(below)**, *the only cactus species native to the East. Loaded with tasty red berries, the American mountain ash* **(left)** *is found at the higher elevations of western Maryland, especially amidst open rocks, where there is less competition for sunlight and nutrients. Loose piles of fragmented shale* **(bottom left)** *create an inhospitable desert-like environment. Shale barrens occur in the ridge and valley province on steep, south-facing slopes, where rainwater quickly drains downhill, leaving little moisture for the nutrient-poor soils to absorb.*

Following pages: *Many a superlative has been lavished upon these rare beauties. The yellow-fringed orchid* **(left)** *is one of some forty-two native orchids to grow in Maryland, while the purple passionflower* **(right)** *has only one cousin here. The flamboyant wild orchids and passionflowers are more commonly associated with the tropics, home to hundreds of outlandish species.*

Above: *The arthritic limbs of an old giant fill the sky. The Wye Oak is the largest white oak in the country; its massive trunk measures thirty-two feet in circumference. Closing in on its 500th birthday, this magnificent oak took root near the village of Wye Mills in Talbot County. As evidenced by the support cables, the Maryland Forest Service lavishes plenty of attention on this particular patient, but wind, ice storms and lightning have taken a heavy toll, especially in the absence of neighboring trees to provide a buffer from the elements.*

Right: *A splash of color makes autumn walks an exhilarating experience. Colder temperatures in the fall trigger the green chlorophyll in leaves to fade, revealing other hues that each leaf contains. No longer able to manufacture energy, the leaves die within a few weeks and fall to the ground, where the color quickly fades to somber shades of brown.*

Following pages: *An aerial view of Assateague Island reveals a variety of habitats, including ocean, beach, dunes, maritime forest, salt marsh, and coastal bay. This fragile and dynamic ecosystem (called a "barrier island") stretches for thirty-seven miles from the Ocean City Inlet to Chincoteague National Wildlife Refuge in Virginia. Assateague once extended into Delaware, but a major storm in 1933 caused a breach, subsequently sealed open by stone jetties to provide boaters ocean access.*

Woodlands burst with color during the annual parade of wildflowers known as springtime ephemerals. By early summer many of these species will have set seed and died back to the ground, leaving no visible trace of the bouquets that carpeted the land only weeks before. Two of the earliest and most common bloomers are bloodroot (below) *and trout lily* (above). *The name "bloodroot" derives from the bright red sap that oozes from its finger-sized root when broken. Trout lily, whose flowers typically point downward, is named for its mottled green and brown leaves, thought to resemble the abstract image of a trout in rippling water. Shooting stars* (left) *are one of nature's best floral representations of bursting fireworks. Though colonies may contain hundreds of plants, they are difficult to find, primarily occurring on limestone bluffs in Washington and Allegany counties.*

Wintertime beauty takes on the fanciful, ever-fleeting forms of snow, ice, and frost. Few sites in nature are as soothing as a blanket of wet snow coating the branches (above)*, but rising temperatures and wind usually make this wintertime wonderland show a brief one. Winter grasses glitter after an infrequent ice storm* (right)*, when rains falling from warmer air above freeze on any object in its path. Though aesthetically pleasing, ice storms are very destructive, as branches and entire trees can snap under the extreme weight of frozen water. Feathery patterns of frost* (below) *decorate a windowpane at dawn. Frost occurs when moisture-rich air crystallizes on surfaces chilled to below freezing, bypassing the liquid stage.*

One of Maryland's most striking features are the Miocene cliffs **(right)** *that extend some thirty miles along Calvert County's eastern shore. Millions of years ago, southern Maryland lay under a shallow ocean, and as marine animals died, their remains settled to the bottom, covered by mud and sand. The exposed cliffs, which peak at over 100 feet, are constantly eroded by wind, rain, and rising Chesapeake tides, yielding the entombed shells, bones and teeth of ancient animals to the surf. Combing the fossil-rich beaches has become a classic Maryland tradition. An abundant supply of shark teeth is the main quarry, and large ones are not uncommon, but this five-inch giant* **(above, on top)** *is the find of a lifetime. It belongs to an extinct species of great white shark that reached a maximum length of fifty feet.*

Above: *A discovery of white trilliums highlights any springtime walk in the woods. Trilliums are so-named for their sets of three leaves, sepals, and petals, though individual plants of a given species may vary from this general pattern. Similar to other wildflowers that grow in colonies, the trilliums' primary means of reproduction is asexual; shoots, called "rhizomes," grow out of a plant's rootstalk, from which new plants can sprout.*

Left: *One of Maryland's best kept secrets is Potomac State Forest, 12,000 acres of picturesque wooded mountains in southern Garrett County. Here several streams flow into the North Branch of the Potomac, including Lost Land Run, an exceptional cascading mountain creek that features a waterfall aptly named Cascade Falls, viewed here during autumn's low flow.*

Following pages: *A spillway on a beaver dam creates a beautiful waterfall which relieves excess pressure on the dam during periods of high water. These marvels of engineering are an increasingly common sight in Maryland. Constructed from simple materials like logs, branches, stones, mud, and leaves, the dams are subjected to tremendous pressure exerted by the impounded water, but they rarely break open, inspected daily by their architects to maintain tip-top performance.*

Above: *The gentle Appalachian Mountains ripple across the landscape, often shrouded in a blue haze. The ridge and valley province of Maryland covers most of Washington and Allegany counties, where numerous north-south ridges are separated by narrow valleys. Maryland's mountains are at least 250 million years old, significantly older than their western counterparts, the Rockies; the Appalachian's once mighty peaks have been erased into mere geologic humps by eons of wind and rain attacking the rock.*

Right and left: *Swallow Falls State Park shelters a magnificent stand of old-growth forest, offering a rare glimpse of Maryland's pre-colonial woodlands. Defined as forests that have never been disturbed (logged) by man, old growth was the predominant habitat in the East before European settlers reshaped the environment. Today less than 1,000 acres of scattered tracts remain, of which Swallow Falls is the only one to be incorporated into a park. This view shows typical old-growth features: a mixture of young and old trees (many of the white pines and eastern hemlocks predate the Declaration of Independence), pockets of deep shade, and an abundance of ferns and mosses growing over the rotting logs and moist, mounded humus that forms the forest floor. It is a setting ideal for fungi, such as these delicate orange mushrooms called salmon entoloma.*

Delightful patterns abound in the natural world; finding them is simply a matter of where one looks. Rainwater pools atop huge leaves of the American lotus **(above)**, *creating an intriguing study of circles. This plant grows in the murky bottoms of shallow ponds and rivers, so it is best viewed from a canoe. A patch of tiny bluets* **(far left)**, *no larger than a maple leaf, is easily overlooked when speeding by a roadside or lawn, the type of open, disturbed habitat that it favors. Brilliant red berries* **(left)** *decorate the branches of winterberry, a deciduous shrub of the holly family that grows in moist thickets. Persisting well into winter's grip on the land, the fruits are an important food source for birds, making it a popular winter garden planting.*

Above: *Each September a high tide of gold rises over freshwater marshes in the form of tickseed sunflowers, which also flourish in old fields and roadsides. Its fruit—the double-pronged sticker which readily attaches to clothes during fall hikes—is no less familiar. The unusual tree in the background is a bald cypress, a deciduous conifer whose needles turn a russet-brown in autumn.*

Left: *An oasis of icicles creates a bizarre landscape, apparently formed from wind-blown mist from a tiny streamlet. When temperatures hover around the freezing point, dripping water freezes into tapering spikes of ice.*

Following pages: *Where land and water meet, the landscape is often pleasing, lush with plant life, including (*clockwise from bottom left*) a profusion of fragrant water lilies; mountain laurel in peak bloom, an American mountain ash recently felled by a beaver, and a backdrop of winter greens—hemlock and rhododendron—along Lost Land Run.*

Above: *An endangered swamp pink wildflower rises against all odds from a forested wetland. This showy member of the lily family is known from only four locations statewide, and perhaps only 100 populations in all, scattered sparingly over seven states. The plant's rarity is partially explained by its specific growing condition: soil that is permanently saturated yet never flooded—an increasingly scarce habitat in heavily-developed Maryland.*

Left: *An aquatic paradise of American lotus takes on an Amazonian mystique. Surrounded by frisbee-sized leaves, the eight-inch pale yellow flower may stand nearly three feet above the water's surface at low tide. A colony of several hundred plants, in full bloom by July, is truly a sight to behold. There are several naturally occurring populations of American lotus along the Sassafras River in Kent County, though the easiest place to view them is at Lily Pons Water Gardens near Frederick.*

Following pages: *The weathered branches of an eastern red cedar frame a mountainous landscape along the Potomac River in Allegany County. These hearty junipers, known for their twisted, fragrant wood, are one of only a few species that can tolerate the extreme conditions of shale barrens. This particular tree has finally succumbed to the rigors of exposure, its bare skeleton a vivid testimony to the inevitable cycle of life.*

Viewed from the sky or roadway, salt marshes are a delight to the eye. Extensive wetlands like these at Blackwater National Wildlife Refuge in Dorchester County (above) *are primarily confined to the lower Eastern Shore. A remarkable diversity of plant and animal life can be found here; as tides rise and fall, a maze of grassbeds, channels, and mudflats is bathed in an assortment of nutrients, minerals, larvae, and other organic matter forming the basis of a complex food chain. Predatory birds like this great blue heron* (left) *are instinctively drawn to this protein factory. Marshes also play a critical role as filters for the Chesapeake Bay, trapping many of the pollutants and excess nutrients generated by human activity that eventually drain from a seven-state watershed.*

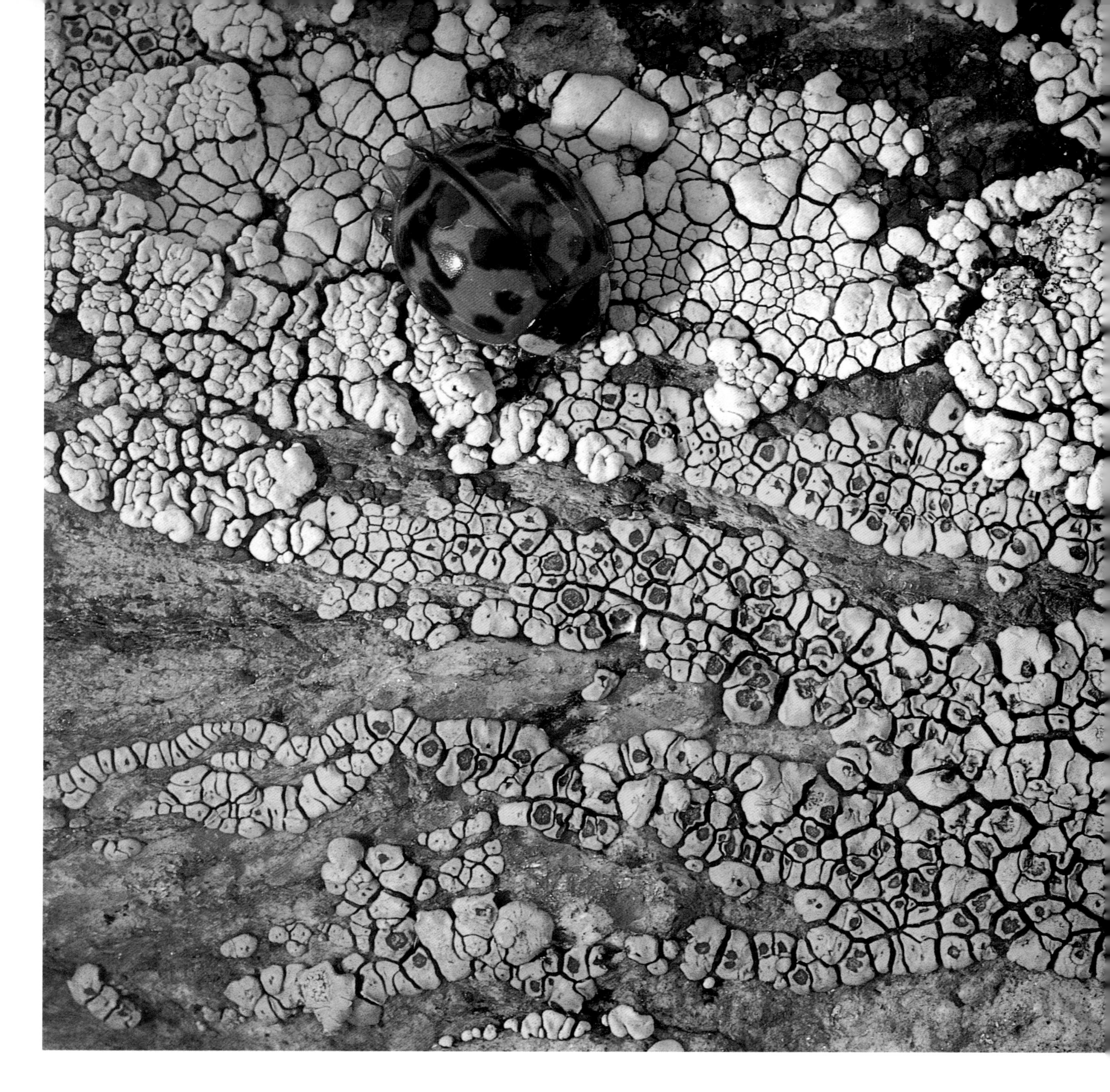

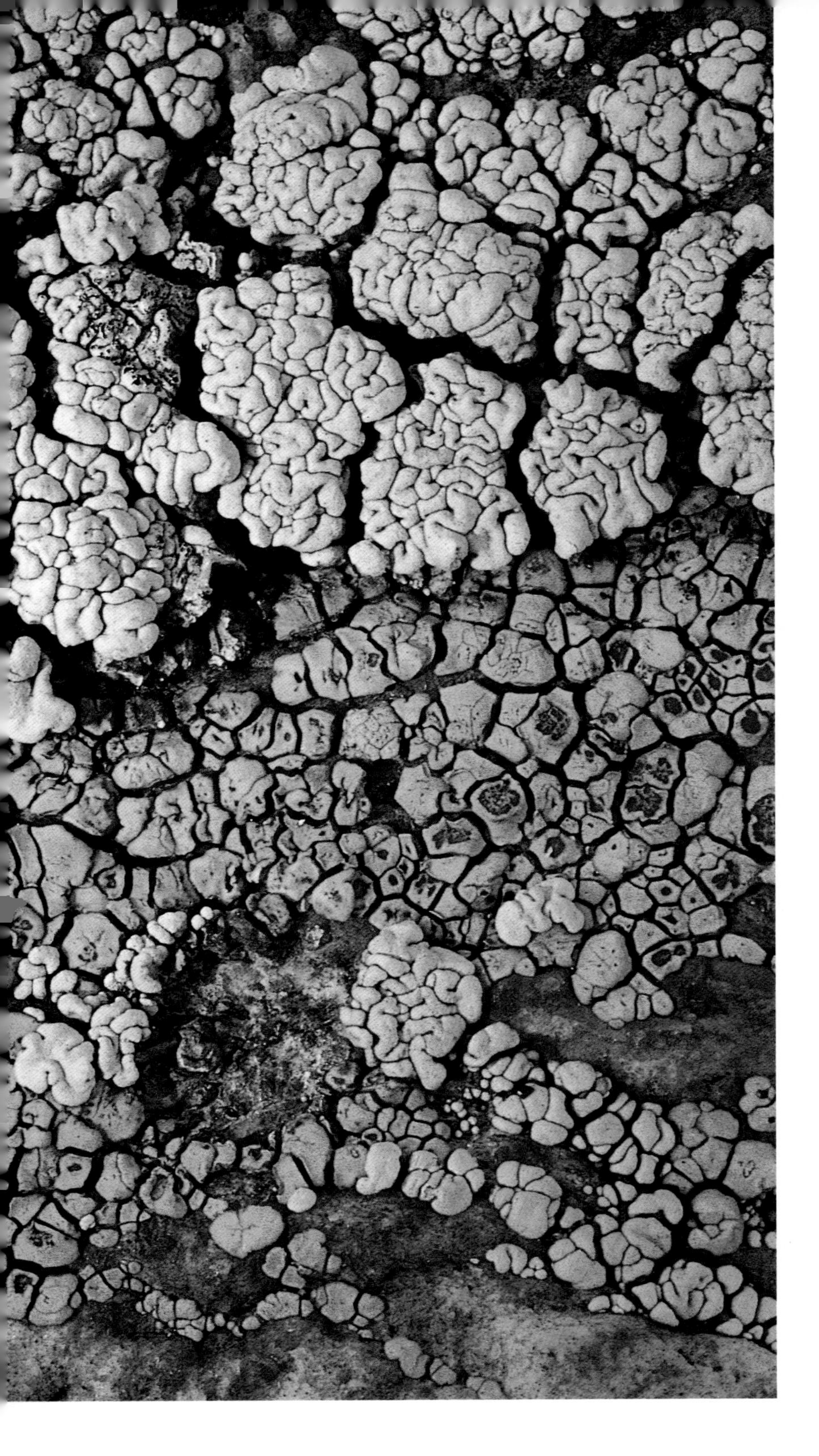

Lichens and fungi come in a variety of shapes, patterns, and colors, as evidenced by these cructose lichens (left), *straight-branched coral* (below), *British soldier lichen* (bottom right), *chicken-of-the-woods* (bottom center) *and edible mushrooms called morels* (bottom left). *Lacking chlorophyll, the green pigment common to all plants, fungi cannot produce their own food, and must therefore absorb their nutrients from other organisms, both living and dead. Lichens are fungi that have formed an interdependent relationship with algae—a primitive family of plants that lack true roots, stems, and leaves, but are capable of photosynthesis.*

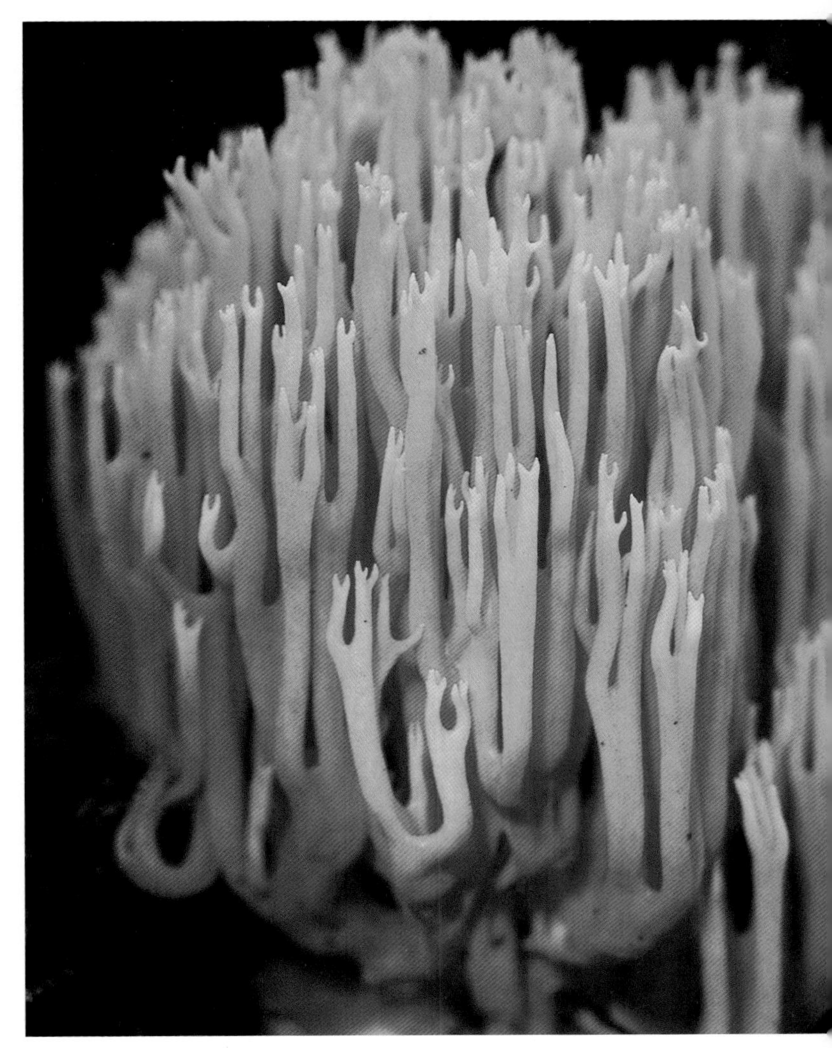

High-quality habitats of ecological significance attract the attention of The Nature Conservancy, an international organization committed to the protection of natural diversity. Founded in 1977, the Maryland/DC Chapter currently owns thirty nature preserves in Maryland, including Battle Creek Cypress Swamp (left) *in Calvert County, the only major stand of bald cypress west of the bay, and Pilot Serpentine Barren in Cecil County, one of only four remaining Serpentine grasslands left in Maryland, where unusual plants like this delicate fameflower* (right) *grow. In addition, the Maryland/DC Chapter has assisted other organizations in the acquisition of wild lands, including Sidling Hill Creek* (above), *a pristine mountain stream valley that runs between Washington and Allegany counties.*

Following pages: *An intimate view of a bog reveals a miniature world of exquisite beauty. Water-logged sphagnum mosses, whose pastel leaves resemble tiny pine cones, serve as a platform on which other plants can grow, including the round-leaved sundew. Its sparkling leaf is about the size of a jelly bean. Sphagnum mosses can absorb many times their weight in water, giving bogs a spongy texture.*

This monochromatic view of Great Falls of the Potomac (left) *contrasts sharply with the floral palette that distinguishes the 185-mile C&O Canal National Historical Park, paralleling the river's north bank from Washington, DC, to Cumberland. In the Great Falls vicinity, a variety of habitats are present, including upland woods, ponds, rocky outcrops, and floodplains. Easy access to these wild lands via the canal towpath brings visitors face-to-face with the display, including* (clockwise from top) *Virginia bluebells, morning glories (white) and trumpet creeper (orange), wild rose, blue flag iris, spring beauty, and wild columbine.*

A scenic overlook in Swallow Falls State Park offers a grand view of the Youghiogheny River **(above and left)** *through the seasons. The picturesque whitewater tumbles not toward the Chesapeake Bay as do other major Maryland rivers, but to the Gulf of Mexico, via the Ohio and Mississippi rivers, an interesting fact explained by the passage of the eastern continental divide along the crest of Backbone and Meadow mountains in Garrett County.*

Wild Creatures

As we go about our daily lives, it is easy to forget that we share the land with myriad forms of life in Maryland. There are subtle reminders—squirrels burying acorns, robins hop-scotching across our manicured lawns, butterflies flitting about the garden, or an unfortunate opossum resting in peace along the roadside. Yet these familiar encounters hardly scratch the surface of the diversity of wildlife species that call this mid-Atlantic enclave home. Because so many creatures are small, nocturnal, secretive, rare, and highly specialized, they seldom cross paths with the average person. Armed with good observation skills, knowledge, and patience, however, anyone can turn a walk in the woods into an eye-opening adventure. The publishing world has responded to America's rekindled interest in ecology with a bounty of insightful narratives featuring natural areas close to home, as well as field guides that enrich our journeys into the wild. Birds lead the parade of nature's ambassadors, easily observed and admired. Adding up the species of wading birds, waterfowl, shorebirds, raptors, songbirds and others, the tally tops 320, of which nearly 200 breed in Maryland. Everyone knows the northern cardinal, wild turkey, and bald eagle, but how about the exquisite scarlet tanager, American oystercatcher, and northern saw-whet owl? Some seventy-five species of mammals occur here; in addition to eastern cottontails and groundhogs, unusual critters like the porcupine, red bat, and an alien called the nutria, eke out a living from the land. The inconspicuous reptiles and amphibians are also well represented, numbering approximately eighty varieties. Mucking through swamps and marshes or lifting up logs, rocks, or discarded carpets and boards may not be glamorous work, but it can be rewarding. Perhaps a spotted turtle, long-tailed salamander, or wood frog will be surprised. Let's not exclude the ubiquitous insects and spiders, integral to the food chain that nourishes our beloved vertebrates. They flaunt many of nature's most flamboyant colors, patterns, and forms; just take a look at the cecropia moth, crab spider, and green darner dragonfly. Round out the smorgasbord with mollusks, crustaceans, and fish, and the spectrum of life found in Maryland can nourish one's visual appetite for the better part of a lifetime.

Preceding pages: *Wildlife from the majestic to the bashful… Snow-white head feathers mark a mature bald eagle. Never one to stand out in a crowd, a pickerel frog hides in a pond covered with duckweed.*

Chesapeake wetlands teem with life. A hatchling diamondback terrapin **(above)** *makes a beeline for the bay across a shell-strewn beach. A male fiddler crab* **(right)** *brandishes his oversized claw, used for dual purposes in courtship and battle, though it is useless against a hungry yellow-crowned night-heron. A close relative, the omnivorous black-crowned night-heron* **(far right)** *emerges in the late afternoon, hunting at the water's edge.*

Nectar is one of nature's most coveted foods, but it is only offered in exchange for pollinating services. While the sweet fluid is consumed, tiny particles of pollen attach to the bodies of insects, hummingbirds, and, in some parts of the country, even bats. As they move from flower to flower, a few grains eventually reach another flower's pistil, ensuring fertilization. The ruby-throated hummingbird **(above)** *is common in gardens across Maryland; it is the only one of North America's sixteen species of hummingbird to breed in the East. A yellowpatch skipper* **(below)** *sips nectar through its long, hollow tongue (called a "proboscis") inserted into a swamp milkweed bloom. Perhaps the most famous pollinator of all is the industrious honey-bee* **(left)**, *which gathers both nectar and pollen, to be stored within the hive's six-sided wax cells.*

Above: *Normally a drooping wing would indicate an injured bird, but this snowy egret is just stretching during an afternoon siesta. It is hard to believe that until the early 1900s, these beautiful long-legged waders were shot for their decorative plumes, used to festoon ladies' hats. Fortunately, bird enthusiasts protested, and the practice was outlawed by 1920.*

Left: *A red-shouldered hawk sets his sights on a rustling in the understory. This raptor is a frequently seen buteo (a broad-winged soaring hawk) which typically hunts fields and woodland edges. A distinctive red breast helps distinguish the red-shouldered hawk from the ubiquitous red-tailed hawk, which sports cream-colored chest feathers.*

Above: *A real prize for snake enthusiasts in Maryland is the coastal plain milk snake, a close relative of the more commonly seen eastern milk snake and the scarlet kingsnake, a southern species which does not occur this far north. Coastals are found sparingly along the Eastern Shore and in southern Maryland; the most spectacular specimens come from St. Mary's County. Milk snakes are constrictors—grabbing their prey (birds, rodents, and other reptiles) and coiling tightly around them until they suffocate. A good-sized meal can nourish a snake for weeks at a time.*

Right: *The rough green snake is a widely distributed, yet seldom seen reptile, named for its keeled scales which are coarse to the touch. More at home in trees, bushes, and vines than on the ground, this agile climber, not much thicker than a pencil, blends in well with surrounding foliage, even on this rather flashy pokeweed plant. Harmless to humans, it hunts for spiders, caterpillars, and other insects.*

Following pages: *A trio of wild ponies seeks relief on the beach from mosquitoes and other biting insects that plague Assateague Island. Currently some 150 ponies—each easily identified by its unique markings—roam the Maryland portion of this barrier island. According to Assateague naturalists, this is a few too many, for they graze prodigiously on grasses critical to the stability of this inherently fragile ecosystem.*

Above: *A most bizarre insect with an otherworldly design is the praying mantis. Laying in wait, it will pounce upon any insect that comes within reach. Its forelegs are lined with sharp spines, and few victims will escape its grasp. Several types of mantis have been introduced to North America, for they are voracious hunters of garden pests.*

Left and below: *Treading a fine line between delicate beauty and the stuff of nightmares, spiders are fascinating creatures. Not all spiders spin webs. This jumping spider* **(below)** *can leap an inch at a time, not bad when you're only the size of a pea. Jumpers have eight eyes—four in front and four smaller eyes on its sides—which provide excellent vision, necessary to active hunters. This enterprising crab spider* **(left)** *has ambushed a nectaring bumble bee on blazing star, an uncommon wildflower which grows on serpentine grasslands.*

Following pages: *Many of Maryland's two dozen species of dabbling and diving ducks are unfamiliar to all but the seasoned naturalist. Several beauties include* **(clockwise from bottom left)** *the American widgeon, hooded merganser, lesser scaup, and northern shoveler. All of these individuals are males, called "drakes," handsome in their breeding plumage. Drab-colored female ducks are often difficult to identify, which suits them well while tending their nests.*

Above: *At first glance, it appears just to be another gray squirrel gorging itself on a bouquet of buds. Upon closer inspection, however, this animal is a little different; a large body, fluffy tail, and pale gray fur help to identify this high-wire specialist as an endangered Delmarva fox squirrel. Historically ranging throughout the Delmarva peninsula, the fox squirrel has dwindled in numbers, its core populations now limited to Dorchester, Talbot, and Queen Anne's counties. Biologists with the Department of Natural Resources are in the midst of a reintroduction program to restore this attractive mammal throughout its former range. They are easily observed at Blackwater National Wildlife Refuge.*

Right: *Always on the lookout for danger, a woodchuck stands upright to get a better view of his world. When alarmed he quickly scampers into a burrow, which is never far away. Groundhogs, as they are commonly called, are frequently seen along roadsides, where there are plenty of greens to eat—few of these rodents starve to death. Many consider the woodchuck to be a pest, for its holes are a danger to livestock (causing broken legs), and it will not hesitate to raid a cropfield or garden.*

Above and below: *A colorful male eastern box turtle attempts to win the affections of a disinterested female. Box turtles possess a unique feature—a hinged lower shell called the "plastron," which can be sealed shut in the face of unwelcomed advances or danger, thus protecting their retractable fleshy appendages. These reptiles are long-lived; a few specimens are reported to be more than a century old. Less durable are turtle eggs, leathery and flexible, which are buried in sand or loose dirt. Once liberated from their shells, hatchlings such as this snapping turtle must dig out of their nesting chamber to the freedom of land, and ultimately, the water.*

Left: *A late arrival to the festivities, a lonely male wood frog is surrounded by a cluster of gelatinous egg masses deposited the night before by dozens of mating frogs. This attractive amphibian species is the first to breed in Maryland, when the trees are still bare in March. Hundreds of wood frogs may gather at a single breeding pond, calling and chasing one another around the clock. In less than a week the commotion is over, and the adult frogs retreat into the woods, where they will forage for beetles and other insects through the fall.*

Perhaps it is the forward-facing eyes, or the swiveling heads, or the fluffy feathers which enable soundless flight, but whatever their unusual characteristics, owls have won our hearts. The monkey-faced barn owl **(left)** *is one of the farmer's best friends; a mated pair may kill 1,000 rats, mice, and voles during a three-month nesting season. Its name reflects a penchant for nesting on man-made structures such as castles, church belfries, and barns. The northern saw-whet owl* **(above)** *is Maryland's cutest bird, standing no more than four or five inches tall. A rare breeding bird of western Maryland, the saw-whet typically nests in coniferous forests to the north but migrates to the mid-Atlantic each fall, where winters are not as harsh. The great horned owl* **(right)** *is common in Maryland, present in virtually every patch of woods. These well-fed siblings have managed to fly atop the tree snag in which their parents nested.*

Following pages: *A sika doe strikes a pose amidst a bed of ferns on Assateague Island, where this introduced species of elk (native to Asia) is easily seen. Unlike whitetails, sika deer will readily take to the open marshes, where they browse on various grasses, though elsewhere they generally inhabit shrub thickets. The adults are distinguished from white-tailed deer by a whitish rump and spots on their backs.*

His signs are everywhere—felled trees ringed with woodchip piles (below right), *dams* (below left), *and ponds brimming with life. A rodent with an engineering degree, the beaver* (left) *has regained a strong foothold since being restocked earlier this century. Except for man, no animal on earth so radically reshapes his environment to suit his own needs. Beavers dam forested streams to create ponds, which provide safety from terrestrial predators. They feed on the bark and leaves of nearby trees, retreating to the pond's safety at the first sign of danger. All of their hard work also benefits a number of other creatures that favor its swampy home. One of several bird species to take up residence is the wood duck* (above), *which feeds and nests in wooded wetlands. Woodies have also staged a dramatic comeback, thanks in part to the installation of man-made nesting boxes.*

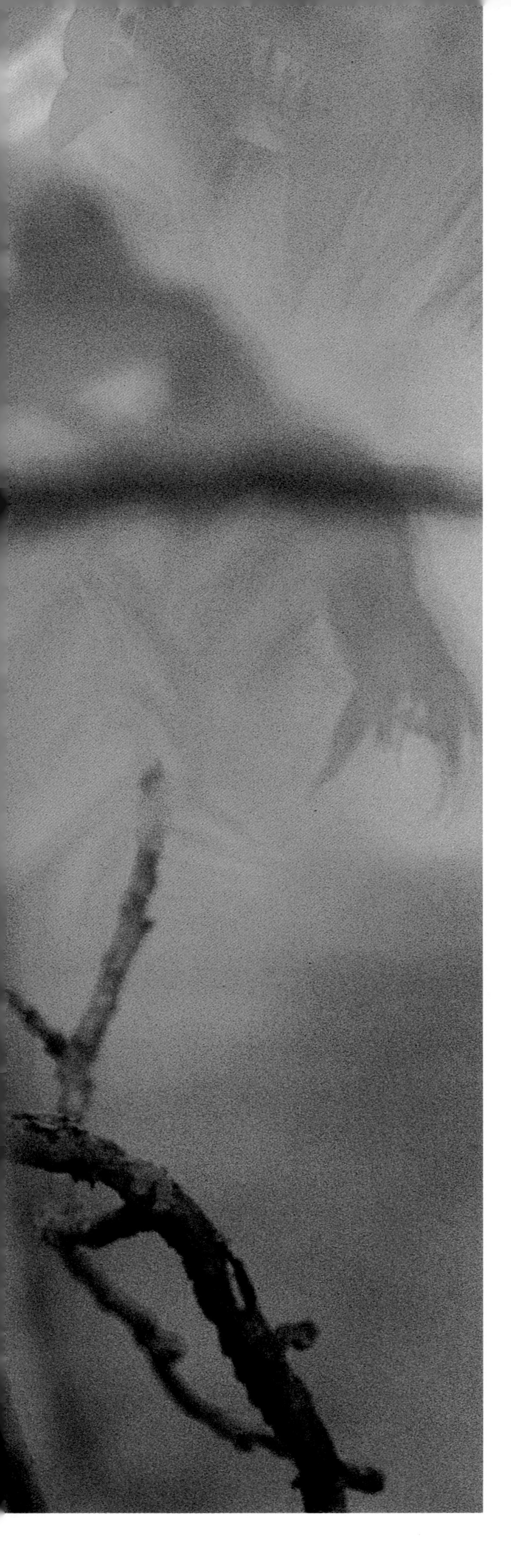

Two of the noisiest birds to inhabit Maryland's wetlands are the red-winged blackbird (above) *and belted kingfisher* (left). *During the breeding season, male red-winged blackbirds call out repeatedly from favorite perches in their territory, stretching their wings to reveal brilliant shoulder patches. Never far away from the marshes where blackbirds nest are the kingfishers, whose loud rattling cry is familiar to all birdwatchers. Just a bit larger than an American robin, the kingfisher feeds on fish, crayfish, frogs, and tadpoles, which they dive-bomb on the wing. Notoriously shy, the kingfisher nests by excavating a tunnel several feet long into a streambank, at the end of which is a nesting chamber shrouded in darkness.*

Dazzling in peak-breeding plumage are the scarlet tanager (above) *and northern parula* (below), *a member of the warbler family. These birds are grouped in with many other songbirds collectively known as "neotropical migrants"—insect-eating, often colorful small birds that migrate each fall to tropical latitudes. The scarlet tanager is especially fond of tent caterpillars* (left)*; individuals have been observed eating scores of these populous larvae in a single feeding. Harbingers of spring, these jewel-like birds have declined dramatically in the past few decades; conservationists are working diligently to identify the culprits in the hope of reversing this trend. One major problem is the clearing and fragmentation of woodlands, as many species only nest successfully in the interior of large tracts of forest, where the nest-parasitic brown-headed cowbird does not venture.*

By late spring, a new generation of youngsters has swollen the food chain. Few animals are as endearing as the raccoon (above)*, especially a group of babies fumbling over a woodpile. Young raccoons are occasionally taken as pets, though the practice is illegal. Raccoons are known carriers of the insidious rabies virus, and adorable adolescents age into temperamental and mischievous adults. Eastern cottontails* (below) *seek refuge in a hollow log from a world full of dangers. Rabbits are prolific breeders; a single female can raise up to six litters a year, each averaging five to seven bunnies. Not surprisingly, mortality rates are extremely high. The burden of motherhood takes on a new meaning for this unique albino Virginia opossum* (left)*, and her fast-growing young will soon have to do their own climbing. The opossum is North America's only marsupial; the bee-sized embryonic newborn must journey to mother's pouch for food and safety, where development continues for another two months.*

Above: *Adopted symbol of Maryland's gentrified countryside, a ring-necked pheasant displays his tail feathers vigorously. Natives of Asia, these large game birds were introduced to the state in the late 1800s, readily populating the rolling farmland of central Maryland. Nonetheless, they have since dwindled in numbers as more agricultural areas are converted to commercial use. Pheasants are now confined to a narrow band from northern Baltimore County west to Washington County.*

Right: *Feathers flared with elegance, a tricolored heron spots her mate, who will take over incubation duties while she fills an empty stomach. Formerly called the "Louisiana heron," this splendid wading bird undergoes an extraordinary transformation at the height of the nesting season—its eyes and legs show a deep purple-red, portions of its bill and lores (bare skin patches around the eyes) turn blue, and its head grows decorative white plumes while golden nuptial feathers cascade down the back. Within weeks the eccentricities will begin to fade, though it is a stunning bird in any form.*

Maryland's waterways are home to a variety of turtles, including the red-eared slider **(right)**, *spotted turtle* **(left)**, *eastern painted turtle* **(bottom left)**, *and an uncommon river cooter* **(bottom right)**. *Though these reptiles spend a majority of their time underwater, they can frequently be seen basking on logs and vegetation on warm, sunny days, energizing their cold-blooded bodies. It is not uncommon to see a dozen or more painted turtles and sliders piled on top of a prime sunbathing perch, but they readily drop into the water when approached. The spotted turtle is more inconspicuous, preferring swamps and wet meadows to open water.*

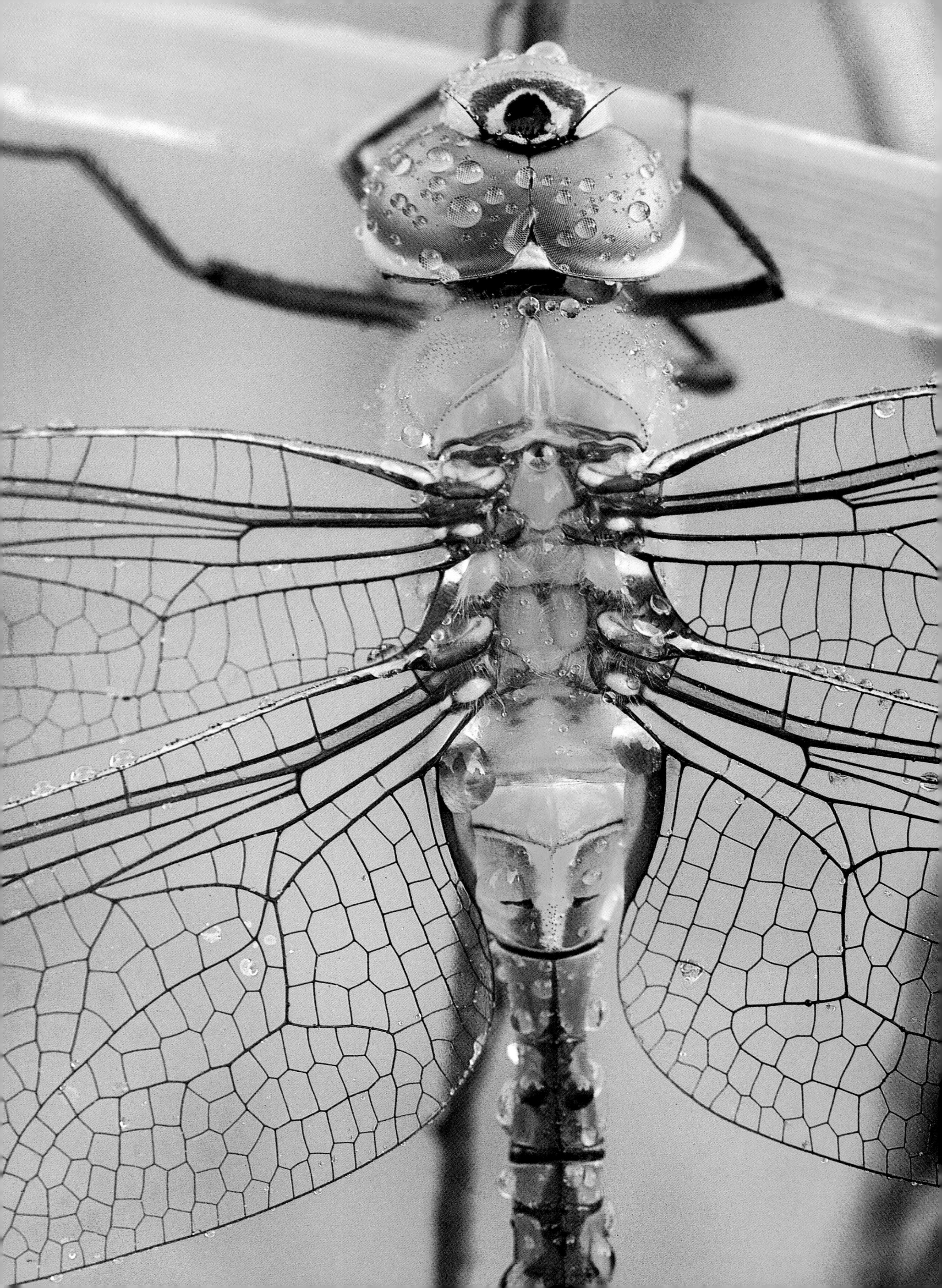

Above: *The intricate markings and colors of a six-lined racerunner are just a blur when these high-energy lizards dart across sandy beaches or rocky outcrops. They are especially active on very hot days; catching one by hand is a most challenging feat. Here a male is basking on a rotten log, also host to a robust colony of British soldier lichen, which prefers a similar hot and dry habitat. Adult racerunners average eight inches in length, much of which is accounted for by its extremely long tail.*

Left: *Scouring meadows on chilly mornings may yield such treats like this green darner dragonfly. A close-up view of this insect reveals exquisite colors and patterns that pass undetected when they patrol ponds and streams for mosquitoes and other winged prey. The green darner has a wingspan of nearly four inches, making it a giant among Maryland's squadron of flying dragons. The four wings can move independently of one another, enabling forward, backward, and hovering flight. The large compound eyes are covered with approximately 40,000 light-sensitive facets, impressive by insect standards, though not nearly as detailed as the human eye's resolution, defined by millions of photosensors.*

Following pages: *A fledgling osprey dines on a catfish while its sibling stretches unskilled wings. For a while after the chicks take their first flight, the parents will continue to provide food at the nest, for it takes practice to master the art of snatching up fish swimming near the surface. By autumn their wings will be put to another test—the annual migration to Latin America.*

Above: *Wild tundra and mute swans (with orange bills) put their differences to rest when free handouts of corn are offered. Despite an overall similar appearance, these are two very different birds. Tundra swans are native, and, like other migratory waterfowl, they breed thousands of miles to the north. Mute swans are indigenous to Europe. In the 1960s several pairs escaped from private collections and readily took to the Chesapeake Bay; now some 2,000 wild mutes have claimed prime habitat on which native waterfowl depend, a problem that concerns wildlife managers.*

Left and below: *The Canada goose is one of our most recognizable birds; a flock honking overhead in classic V-formation is a sure sign that winter is approaching. Though the total state population of non-migratory geese is increasing, the number of truly wild Atlantic flyway birds has dropped off in recent years, due to excessive hunting and a series of poor breeding seasons in northern Canada. Many of the Canada geese in Maryland currently are year-round residents, descendants of a different strain of goose (there are more than ten subspecies) that were released here and have since flourished, congregating along municipal parks, golf courses, and the suburbs, creating somewhat of a nuisance.*

There's nothing like the inquisitive stare of white-tailed deer during woodland hikes (left) *to reconnect us instantly to nature, and to remind us that the land which we have tamed was once a wilderness where big animals reigned supreme. Healthy bucks such as this eight-pointer* (right) *are especially inspiring; the antlers are shed after the breeding season in late fall, and a new set will begin to grow by spring. Twin fawns such as this pair* (above) *have become commonplace in recent years. Sightings of whitetails are so frequent in Maryland today that it is hard to believe that just a half-century ago they were nearly extinct in all but the westernmost portions of the state. Restocked in eastern counties, they have rebounded so strongly that in many areas deer are considered a nuisance, raiding gardens, orchards, crops, and creating a nighttime driving hazard. Despite an annual harvest in excess of 50,000 animals, Maryland herds are still growing, which is unhealthy for their habitat, and ultimately, for themselves, stressing the land's carrying capacity.*

An excellent variety of wildlife makes Assateague Island one of Maryland's premier nature retreats. One secretive resident is the ghost crab **(bottom)***, which feeds at night, scurrying along the beach for tidbits of food churned up by the tides. The fabled wild ponies* **(right)** *are the main draw, and friendly as they may appear, visitors are asked not to pet or feed the ponies, which would reinforce their bad habit of frequenting roadways. A common snake on the island is the eastern hognose* **(bottom right)***, a toad-eater which makes a good living here. The black skimmer* **(below)** *uses its long knife-like lower mandible to slice across the water's surface when fishing.*

Above and left: *The Baltimore oriole sports some of the flashiest attire in town, but only the adult males flash a bright yellow-orange. Though it is Maryland's official state bird, the oriole is generally elusive compared to other likely candidates for the distinction, such as the great blue heron or osprey. The telltale nest is a hanging woven basket, usually built on the end of a branch high up in a large tree. A carefully placed orange slice may yield a good view of the bird, as orioles are known to have a sweet tooth.*

Right: *A picture-perfect Baltimore checkerspot awaits warming rays of the morning sun to provide energy for flight. This spectacular butterfly is also named in honor of Cecil Calvert, founding father of colonial Maryland, whose family coat of arms bears the same striking combination of black and orange. Unfortunately, the Baltimore checkerspot is a challenge to find in the wild, for its main host plant, turtlehead, is not very common, and this species does not regularly visit other flowers.*

For these frogs, out on a limb is all in a day's work. Five species of treefrogs can be found in Maryland, including the common gray treefrog (above) *and green treefrog* (bottom right). *Though they congregate at breeding ponds in the spring like other frogs, treefrogs spend most of their time aloft, hunting for insects in the evening. Their large toepads secrete a sticky mucous which allows them to cling to even the smoothest of surfaces. The most famous climbing frog in Maryland is the thumbnail-sized spring peeper* (top right), *so named for its incessant springtime vocalization.*

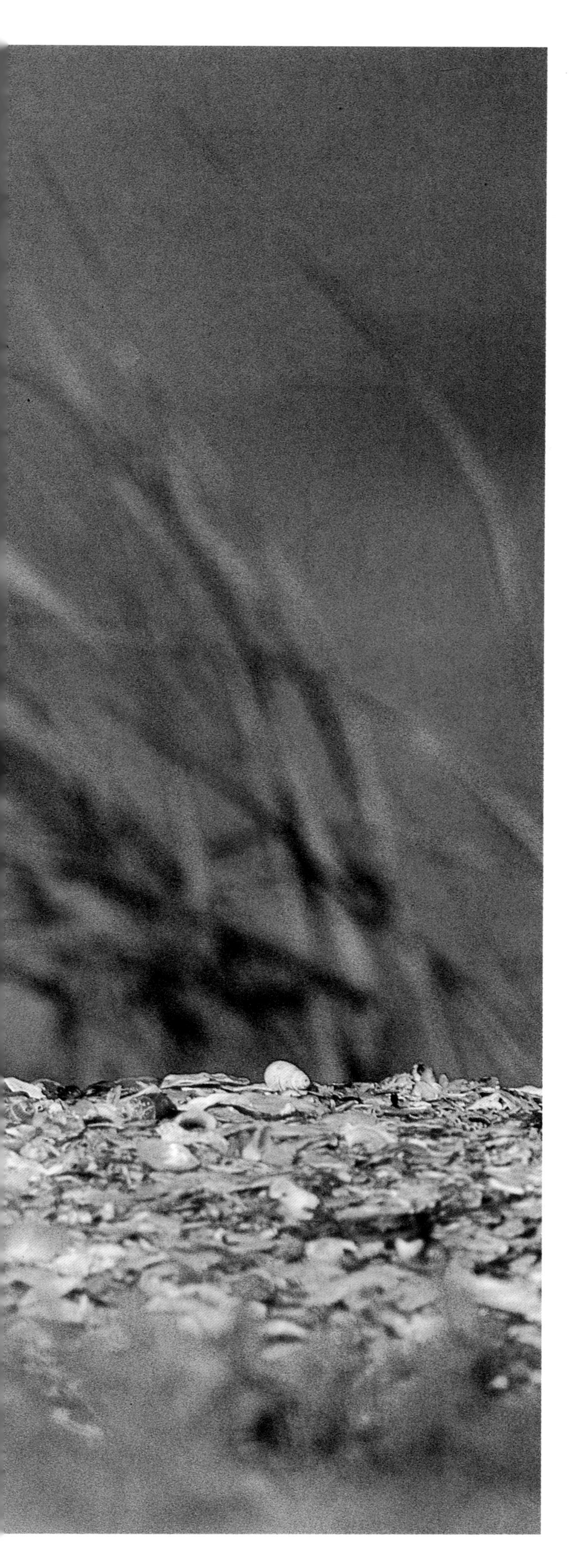

Above: *Many a fish has passed through the gaping mouth of this double-crested cormorant, which accelerates toward its prey underwater with powerful thrusts of webbed feet and wings. A hooked bill affords a good grasp on its slippery catch, that can be regurgitated to feed hungry chicks. Only in a close-up view like this is it possible to appreciate the exquisite turquoise eyes of this accomplished fisherman.*

Left: *An American oystercatcher patrols his turf with moxie. Though these shorebirds are fairly common along the lower Eastern Shore, they require undisturbed beaches for nesting, steering clear of the public eye. As its name implies, the oyster-catcher is a shellfish eater; the flattened tips of its beautiful bill are perfectly designed to pry open bivalves, though it also probes the sand and mud for marine worms.*

Above: *A lonesome Maryland porcupine arches his back, a sure sign of agitation. These bristly critters possess a unique defense system—some 30,000 barbed quills from head to toe, which easily detach and penetrate the skin of an offender who dares to make contact. Porcupines are surprisingly slow and clumsy, especially in trees, where they eat bark, twigs, and buds. This is an animal of the American West and northern forests; it reaches its southern limit on the East Coast along the Maryland-Pennsylvania border. Any sighting of a rare animal such as this should be reported to Department of Natural Resources Wildlife and Heritage Division, as the information is useful to biologists and very much appreciated.*

Right: *At the first sign of danger, the gray fox readily scampers up a tree for safety; it is the only canine in North America that is a skilled climber. Though present in many of Maryland's forests, the gray fox is seldom observed compared to its famous cousin, the red fox. Grays prefer secluded woodlands for hunting and denning, rarely venturing out into the open. There is debate as to whether or not reds were present in Maryland before colonization. There is no doubt, however, that frustrated fox hunters from England, learning of the gray fox's arboreal ways, imported red foxes from Europe to insure the thrill of the hunt.*

Following pages: *Locked in a nuptial embrace, cecropia moths make the most of a very brief life. Lacking true mouthparts and digestive systems, most species of moth rely on stored energy in their chunky bodies to fly, mate, and, in the case of the females, deposit eggs on the appropriate host plant. The male* (on left) *has extremely large feathery antennae, capable of detecting the scent of females a mile away.*

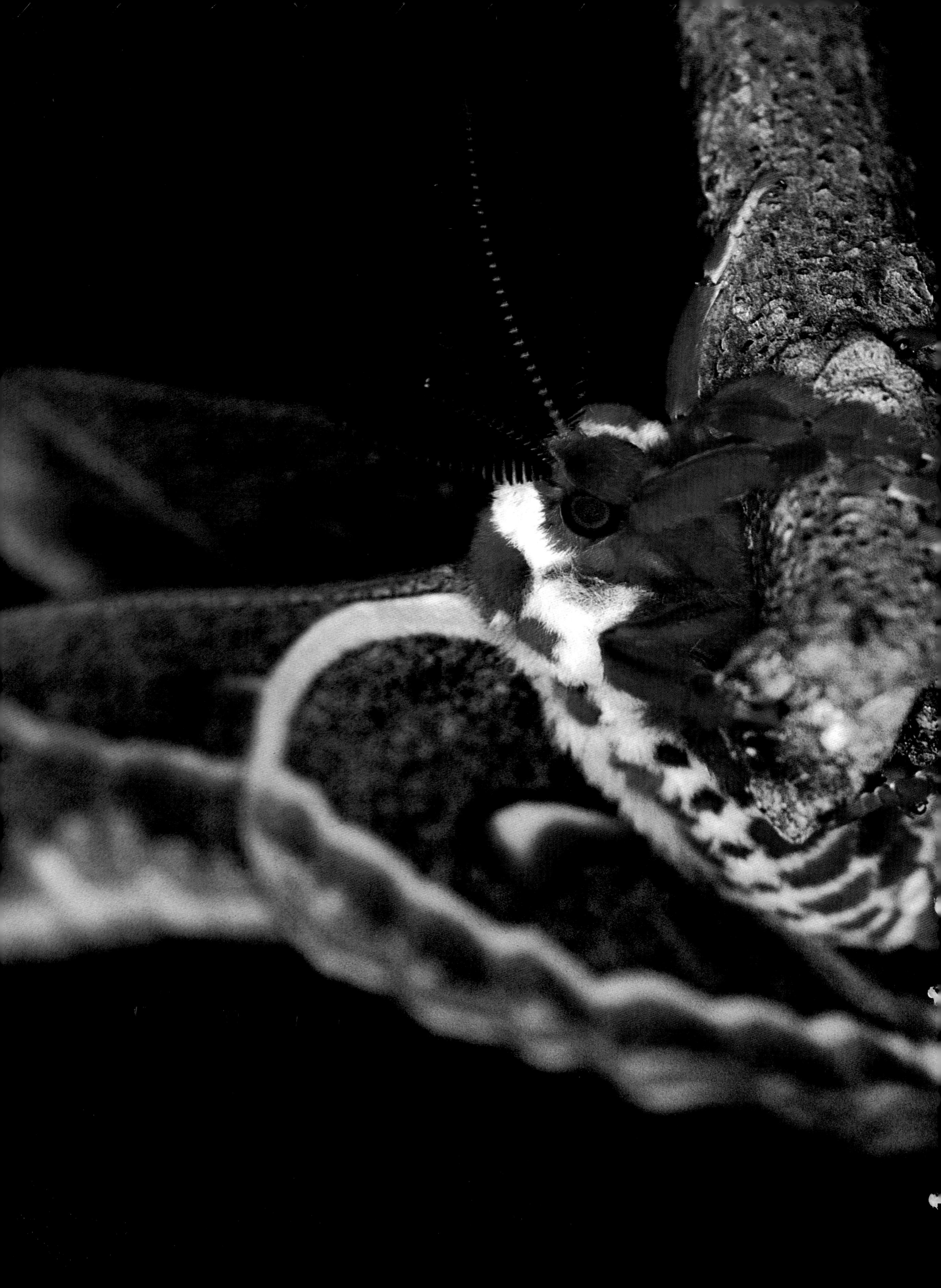

Unlike classic birds of prey, which tear flesh with hooked bills, waterbirds must consume their food whole. Once in a while a highly prized catch must be relinquished because it simply will not fit through the bird's mouth. Within minutes of spearing a vole, this great blue heron (right) *swallowed it, still wiggling as it traveled down the heron's elongated neck. An immature great black-backed gull* (above) *looks a bit perplexed with this unusually-shaped fish, called a "lookdown," which was eventually folded in half before disappearing into the gull's mouth. This great egret* (below) *would have an easy time devouring the eel if it were not for a pesky snowy egret (yellow feet) trying to steal it away.*

Above: *A pair of diamondback terrapins make for handsome ambassadors, selected as the mascot for the University of Maryland. Nearly fished to extinction early this century to satiate the public's demand for terrapin soup, diamondbacks have made a strong recovery, but threats still remain. Shoreline development disrupts traditional nesting beaches, and they easily drown in crab pots, unable to hold their breath for more than a few hours at a time. Terrapins hunt for small fish, snails, and crustaceans in brackish and saltwater margins of estuaries.*

Right: *One of Maryland's most unusual fish is the lined seahorse, which inhabits the Chesapeake and coastal bays of Worcester County. Not only does it swim upright, fluttering its dorsal fin, but the seahorse reproduces in a most unusual way. Females deposit their eggs in a brood pouch on the male's belly, where fertilization occurs. Several weeks later the male "gives birth," squeezing out the tiny replicas. Not particularly strong swimmers, seahorses prefer waters laced with aquatic vegetation, to which they anchor, curling their tails around grasses swaying in the tides.*

Above: *The nutria bears a strong resemblance to the beaver; it is big, brown, aquatic, and toothy, yet it lacks the paddle tail. Nutrias are native to South America, brought into the United States to be commercially farmed for its fur. Released or escaped, nutrias are now living wild on Maryland's lower Eastern Shore, chewing up large tracts of sensitive Chesapeake wetlands. Consequently, they are targeted for eradication.*

Right: *A raft of canvasback ducks can cause quite a bit of commotion when a cache of food is discovered. Though this image may imply a bounty of canvasbacks in Maryland, the truth is less heartening; current populations are a mere fraction of their heyday decades ago, when they descended on the Chesapeake Bay each fall in uncountable numbers. The primary culprit has been a precipitous decline of their staple food—submerged aquatic vegetation, particularly wild celery.*

A rufous-sided towhee **(above)**, *now referred to as the "eastern towhee," displays a look of concern, as does this handsome cedar waxwing* **(below)**. *When alarmed, songbirds engage in an unusual behavior called "mobbing." Instead of fleeing from the haunting calls of an owl, for example, they converge on the source of danger and try to drive him away, calling loudly and whizzing by their eternal enemy. Several raptors specialize in songbird hunting, including the Cooper's hawk* **(right)**. *This particular bird is an adult, with slate-gray plumage and ruby eyes. The medium-sized Cooper's, and its smaller look-alike, the sharp-skinned hawk, frequently patrol the busy corridors near bird feeders, thus explaining the nervous behavior of songbirds there.*

Bats, spiders, and snakes—just mentioning the words can elicit strong feelings of fear, panic, and disgust. Pictured here are the red bat (below), *eastern garter snake* (above), *and black-and-yellow argiope* (left). *Many myths have arisen, perhaps to justify our persecution of these animals, yet there is often little truth to them...snakes are not slimy (amphibians, not reptiles, have smooth, moist skin), bats are not blood-sucking vampires (the species in Maryland are insect-eating), and spiders do not readily bite people (all but a few local species are benign to humans). Consider a world without these predators; we would be overrun by mice, rats, mosquitoes, and other pests. A single bat may consume hundreds of insects in a single hour, sparing many bug bites.*

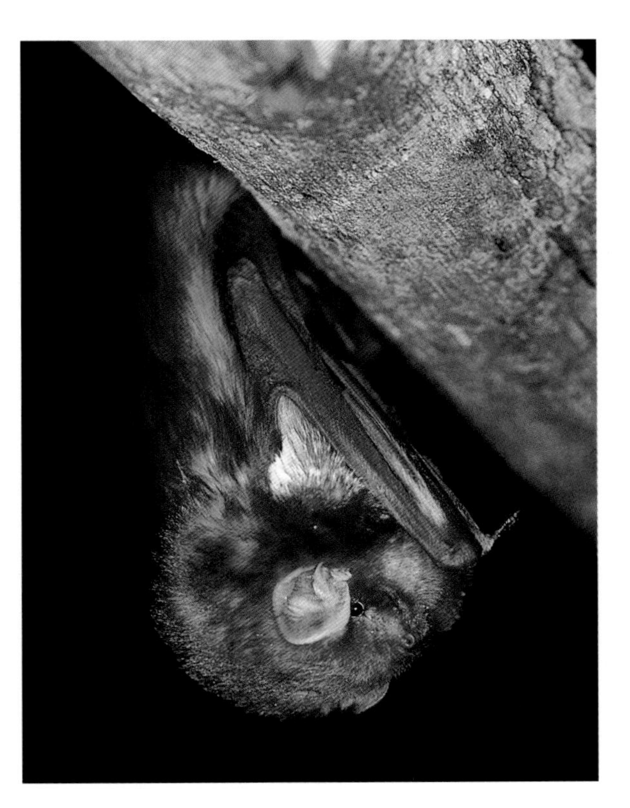

Above: *A dashing zebra swallowtail perches under dense cover for its nighttime roost. Like many other species of butterfly, this winged gem is short-lived; in a week or two it will have succumbed to nature's laws, but a new generation will already be in place—scores of tiny eggs attached to pawpaw leaves. The attractive antennae-like "tails" which make swallowtails so easy to identify serve to divert the attention of marauding birds away from more vital parts of the body.*

Right: *Streambeds are an excellent place to find butterflies, in this case a red-spotted purple. Besides drinking nectar from flowers, butterflies are also attracted to damp places, where deposits of minerals and nutrients are left behind by evaporating water. By excreting saliva through their proboscis onto rocks, they can slurp up chemicals that help fuel daily activities. Many species of butterfly do not gather nectar at all, relying entirely on alternative sources of food, including animal dung.*

Following pages: *Though quite common, lizards and salamanders are among Maryland's most secretive animals. Pictured are* **(clockwise from lower left)** *the red-spotted newt, five-lined skink, eastern fence lizard, and long-tailed salamander. Lizards favor hot and dry habitats such as shale barrens and sandy woodlands dominated by oak and pine, while salamanders are creatures of damp places, living cryptically beneath rocks, log and leaves, and in streams and ponds.*

Common birds of uncommon beauty that add spice to the drabness of winter include the mourning dove **(far right)**, *blue jay* **(above)**, *and northern cardinal* **(right)**. *All are easily attracted to backyard feeders, where their different personalities become evident. Doves are gentle and very social, feeding and roosting together in large groups of a dozen or more all winter long. Blue jays, on the other hand, are noisy and quarrelsome, always announcing their arrival at a feeder; smaller songbirds will generally avoid crossing paths with a jay. Cardinals are the true romantics; they mate for life and stay together throughout the seasons. When one visits a feeder, the other is never far behind.*

Though our wetlands are filled with frogs and toads, they are often difficult to spot, even conspicuous singers like this American toad (above), *broadcasting his amorous intentions under the cover of darkness. Since amphibians are the target of many predators—snakes, egrets, herons, owls, hawks, raccoons, minks, and even larger bullfrogs* (left)*—they remain hidden much of the time. As hunters, toads and frogs must also keep a low profile, ambushing prey that swims, hops, or flies by, swatting it with their long sticky tongues, attached at the front of the mouth. The frog hidden under the grass* (right) *is a leopard frog.*

Following pages: *With a near-deafening cacophony, a flock of snow geese takes flight at Blackwater National Wildlife Refuge, a favorite Eastern Shore haunt. An estimated 100,000 snow geese migrate to the Chesapeake Bay each fall from arctic breeding grounds, feeding over a patchwork of agricultural fields. Traveling in such tight quarters, it is a wonder that they do not knock each other out of the sky.*

Above: *Newly hatched black skimmers await the arrival of their sibling on a hot beach near Ocean City. Like other types of shorebirds, their nest is a simple depression in the sand. For safety they must rely on camouflage and their attentive parents, who rarely leave them unattended. Predatory gulls, which often nest on the periphery of the colony, are a constant threat. Repeated disturbance to nesting beaches by humans can be devastating to a colony of waterbirds, as the young can quickly overheat without shading by their parents. Thus the public is asked by the Department of Natural Resources to refrain from visiting these sensitive areas during the breeding season.*

Right: *An unmistakable silhouette gives away this green treefrog on the move. By day, green treefrogs typically rest motionless on emergent vegetation along the edges of ponds, streams, and marshes, tucked in to minimize moisture loss through evaporation.*

Living in a world full of hungry birds and other predators, butterflies and moths employ a variety of clever strategies to get by. During daylight hours, the splendid pale-green luna moth (left) *perches motionless on tree trunks, branches, and leaves, camouflaging well in summer's sea of green. Regrettably, populations of this and other giant silk moth species have declined as of late, the apparent victims of gypsy moth pesticide, which indiscriminately kills a host of native caterpillars. This rather comical spicebush swallowtail larva* (above) *wears false eyespots designed to intimidate and confuse would-be predators. A newly-hatched pipe-vine swallowtail* (right) *perches inconspicuously while its wings harden and abdomen straightens. Its larvae eat toxic pipe vines; birds will instinctively avoid this species to ward off an upset stomach. Scientists state that such bold wing patterning (also exhibited by the monarch) advertises its distastefulness.*

Above: *A proud turkey struts on his stage, hoping to charm hens into his harem. Thanks to reintroduction efforts by the Department of Natural Resources, the classic gobble of wild turkeys may be heard in every Maryland county once again. Sporting a fan-like tail, outstretched wings, puffed-up iridescent plumage, and colorful fleshy growths on his head (called "carnucles"), a strutting tom is life at its most vigorous. Yet the conspicuous lovesick gobbler is a formidable challenge to the hunter, who can attest to the bird's exceptional alertness and elusive ways.*

Right: *A young black bear seeks refuge in a tree, one of many survival lessons this cub will learn from its doting mother. In recent years, sightings of black bears have become a frequent occurrence in western Maryland. Weighing up to 400 pounds, black bears once roamed across all of Maryland, but as the land was cleared, they became confined to remote tracts of undisturbed habitats in Allegany and Garrett counties. Nearly hunted to extinction in Maryland, a ban was imposed in 1949, and the remaining handful of bears have repopulated steadily; a current estimate of the local population is 200 individuals, though still limited to western Maryland. Unlike its western cousins, the black bear is a shy animal and will generally avoid a confrontation with man. Nonetheless, cubs should never be approached, as mother is always nearby.*

Various faces from the animal world make excellent poster children for the conservation movement. A red-eyed male box turtle (right) *retracts his long neck when confronted by a nosy photographer. An inquisitive long-eared owl* (far right) *makes for an unforgettable face-to-face encounter. The elongated ear tufts actually play no role in hearing, nor are the owl's ear openings located there; these feathers are simply for show, good indicators of a bird's mood. A pudgy raccoon* (below) *gives corn-on-the-cob a try. Nimble forepaws allow raccoons to dine from a large menu, including frogs, fish, crayfish, bird's eggs, nuts, berries, earthworms, insects, and, regrettably, the aromatic contents of a sealed garbage can.*

Above: *Of Maryland's two dozen or so species of snakes, there are only two to avoid—the northern copperhead* **(bottom)** *and timber rattlesnake* **(top)**. *Whereas copperheads are found statewide, timbers are limited to the remote woodlands of western Maryland. Both species are members of the pit viper family; a pair of small holes in front of the eyes are highly sensitive heat detectors which aid in the location of prey. Though the venom is potent, a bite to humans is rarely fatal, though painful beyond words. Mild-mannered, they will strike only when unduly threatened or harassed. In decline, the timber rattlesnake is now protected by law.*

Right: *Weighing in at an average of thirty pounds, the surprisingly dainty bobcat is nonetheless a ball of fire, quite capable of felling an adult deer. Typical prey include rabbits, squirrels, and mice. Though bobcats are well-entrenched in Maryland's mountains, they are notoriously shy, and those lucky enough to see one usually catch only a fleeting glimpse. Like many predators, their senses of smell, hearing, and sight are highly acute, and therefore they are virtually impossible to approach.*

This water-level view of a bullfrog **(above)** *illustrates a trait common to many frogs—bulging eyes atop their heads, a configuration that permits a nearly global field of vision. This is a handy adaptation when one lives in constant fear of predators, including the American bittern* **(top left)** *and green heron* **(bottom left)**. *When alarmed, the "prince of the pond" puffs up by sucking in air, making it more difficult for wading birds to swallow him whole.*

A pair of monarch butterflies (right) *alights on goldenrod, a favorite source of nectar. The larva* (above) *is very distinct and easily found on milkweed plants. When fully grown, the caterpillar anchors itself to a leaf and hangs upside-down. After shedding its skin for the last time, the caterpillar transforms into a jade-colored chrysalis, with its signature gold dots. About two weeks later the dissolved larva has metamorphosed into a tightly folded butterfly, which then cracks through the protective shell, climbs to a perch, and pumps fluid through its veins to flatten its crumpled wings.*

Following pages: *These are happy days for the bald eagles and ospreys that nest along the Chesapeake Bay and hunt its fish. Both birds of prey were nearly wiped out as recently as the 1960s by the pesticide DDT, which weakened eggshells to the point where they would crack under the weight of an incubating parent. Since DDT was banned in 1972, eagles and ospreys have staged an impressive recovery; there are approximately 180 active eagle pairs in Maryland and some 1,500 osprey pairs.The more numerous "fish hawk" frequently nests on structures like duck hunting blinds and channel markers.*

Waterbirds of many designs and colors make the coastal bays near Ocean City a premier birding destination. A treat to the eye is the common loon **(below)** *in breeding plumage, pictured here in April, when they head north to New England and Canada. The rock jetties and pilings at the Ocean City Inlet are great places to spot the ruddy turnstone* **(far left)**. *A large colony of royal terns* **(left)**, *and a rare pair of sandwich terns (with yellow-tipped bills) nest just north of the Route 50 bridge on a protected island. Brown pelicans* **(bottom)** *can be seen flying single-file along the Atlantic beaches. The glossy ibis* **(bottom left)** *is named in recognition of it spectacular iridescent plumage, beautifully complemented by a decurved bill.*

Enjoying Nature

In the "Land of Pleasant Living" there are myriad ways to recreate in nature's realm, to seek relief from the constraints of endless deadlines, household chores, unpaid bills, traffic, and the responsibilities of family life, work, and school, which consume so much of our time. Hit the trails or dip a paddle, and for a small price we can all experience nature through a child's wondrous eyes, with not a care in the world except to investigate a rustling sound in the leaves, or to discover what lies just around the river's next bend. Whether an interest is taken in harvesting natural resources, the thrill of adventure sports, supporting conservation efforts, observing plants and animals in their natural setting, or simply getting some exercise, Maryland's wild lands can soothe our frazzled nerves every month of the year. Some of our most invigorating feelings—renewal, hope and amazement—are deeply rooted in the land. The state's compact borders embrace all sorts of outdoor activities within a two-hour drive for a majority of its populace—fly-fishing on blue-ribbon trout streams, climbing amidst picturesque rock formations, rambling along mountain trails, racing yachts on open water, canoeing pristine freshwater marshes, scouring beaches for shark teeth, or watching a wintertime gathering of bald eagles. We may not have the magnificent rainforests of the Pacific Northwest, the awe-inspiring red-rock canyons and towers of the desert Southwest, the glacial lakes of New England, or the primeval swamps of the deep South, but if year-round variety close to home is the ticket, then much of America can be envious of Marylanders. Very few 10,000 square-mile swatches of this country offer more diversity of plant and animal life, or a full dose of each of the four seasons (which many Marylanders love to complain about). There are hundreds of miles of canoeable creeks, fifty state parks and forests, thirty-seven wildlife management areas, thirty Nature Conservancy preserves, at least a dozen nature centers, a handful of national parks, and several nature clubs and conservation organizations. Wild places are surprisingly close to home, and opportunities to enjoy the natural world abound. Despite a flurry of headlines of environmental loss from all parts of the globe, including our own, much remains to be appreciated and preserved for that child who lives in all of us, as well as in future generations.

Above: *An old salt from Smith Island proudly shows off two large male crabs, called "jimmies," sure to be served up at some restaurant by day's end. The Chesapeake Bay blue crab is Maryland's last great fishery; upwards of 50 million pounds of the cantankerous crustaceans are harvested commercially each year, while recreational crabbers add a significant catch. Efforts are underway to prevent a population collapse—the fate of striped bass, American shad, and the oyster. The subject of much scientific study, the blue crab is still shrouded in mystery; just listen to seasoned watermen recounting tales of its legendary unpredictability. One thing is certain about the blue crab—the sheer pleasure of catching, cooking, and eating it is a common thread that links Marylanders from all walks of life.*

Right: *A longnose gar fish has met its match, an angler armed with bow and arrow. Reaching maximum lengths of five feet, these unusual fish of the lower bay feed along freshwater and brackish rivers, clamping down on prey with long jaws armed in razor-sharp teeth. Though gars may be caught with a baited hook, bow hunting is a popular method of harvest, especially in late spring when these giants congregate at the shallow upper reaches of tidal spawning streams.*

Preceding pages: *Adventures from the deep-freeze of January to the sweltering heat of July... A thoroughly chilled ice fisherman awaits the bite of yet another yellow perch. The frigid Atlantic surf and balmy beaches offer contrasting delights to the senses.*

Numerous hiking and canoeing trails in Maryland provide total immersion in the natural world. River-scoured rock formations along the Billy Goat Trail (right) *create an interesting obstacle course. Accessed from the C&O canal towpath near Great Falls, it is arguably the state's finest nature trail, offering sanctuary for a variety of plants, animals, and landscapes. A first-rate canoeing venue is the Eastern Shore's Pocomoke River and its feeder creeks, where bald cypress trees line the banks, as seen here along Nassawango Creek* (lower right). *The cascading waters of Cunningham Falls* (below) *offer a refreshing break from steep hiking trails in the Catoctin Mountains of Frederick County. Located just a short drive away from the state's core population center, Cunningham Falls State Park affords a convenient glimpse into classic mountain habitat.*

Maryland's wilderness is the subject of many a field trip. Meredith Creek (below) *in Anne Arundel County is one of many sites incorporated into the Chesapeake Bay Foundation's Environmental Education Program. Hands-on experiments like lifting a seine net familiarize students with the bay's plentiful aquatic life. Kids aboard the ninety-six-foot* Lady Maryland (above and following pages) *enjoy the thrill of traditional sailing while discussing the bay's ecology, economy, and maritime history. This recreated pungy schooner sails as flagship for the Baltimore-based Living Classrooms Foundation. On a wooded hillside near the Irvine Natural Science Center* (left), *youngsters discover how native Americans made a living from the land. Based on the campus of St. Timothy's School in Baltimore County, Irvine promotes environmental awareness and appreciation to Marylanders of all ages through a host of nature-related activities, seminars and exhibits.*

LIFE JACKETS
5 ADULT
30 CHILD

Above and below: *Intent on avoiding consumption, a northern puffer instinctively sucks in air, and quite a mouthful it is. Fortunately for the fish, its captors are state fisheries biologists. Since 1975 the same twenty scattered sites between the Delaware and Virginia state lines have been sampled regularly as part of an ongoing coastal bay research project. Every captured puffer, flounder, crab, and countless other marine animals are logged. Over the years many unusual fish have been netted from Assawoman, Isle of Wight, Sinepuxent, and Chincoteague bays, including this spotfin butterflyfish.*

Left: *Fisheries personnel search a holding pen for American shad, a savory fish poised for a comeback. This fish lift is located at the Conowingo Dam along the Susquehanna River, fourteen miles upstream from the Chesapeake Bay. Shad attempting to reach traditional spawning grounds upriver are blocked by this and several other dams, so a fish lift has been installed to address the problem. American shad captured here during the spring spawning season are trucked daily to the Susquehanna's headwaters in Pennsylvania, where nature can resume its course.*

Above: *A tipsy sycamore tree and a discarded piece of rope make a great way to beat the dog days of summer. Maryland's swimming holes are secrets often passed from one generation to the next, and the fact that they are often unauthorized makes it all the more fun.*

Left: *Parasailing is the latest in a wave of watersports to hit Ocean City, offering adventurous souls a bird's-eye view of the beach from 150 feet above the ocean. To conclude a flight, one is simply reeled in by a large spool, just like a feisty marlin.*

The spectacular fifty-two-foot Muddy Creek Falls (left), *the highest in Maryland, highlights a trip to Swallow Falls State Park in western Garrett County. In wintertime the rock face behind the falls is usually encrusted with icicles, as are several rocky ledges under which the main trail passes. Both this creek and Tolliver Run empty into the Youghiogheny River just downstream, which itself offers a splash of whitewater as the river drains through a scenic gorge. Visitors looking for a more vigorous workout may cross-country ski* (above) *on hiking trails which pass through the old-growth forest.*

MARYLAND

It can be a messy job, but the work must get done.... Field biologists with the Department of Natural Resources Wildlife and Heritage Division locate and monitor hundreds of rare plant and animal species, in addition to threatened habitats. A botanist (above) *photographs one of the state's two remaining colonies of Indian paintbrush, a beautiful wildflower more commonly associated with the West. At John Friend Cave* (right) *in Garrett County, a subterranean stream is examined for tiny invertebrates. In 1992 a new species of cave-dwelling beetle was discovered here and in nearby Crabtree Cave, both owned by The Nature Conservancy. Two barn owlets* (left) *await the indignity of banding at their nest box on the vast salt marshes of the lower Eastern Shore. Here their populations are being bolstered to offset the decline of barn owl populations across Maryland's farmland, dotted with a dwindling supply of old barns, which make ideal nest sites.*

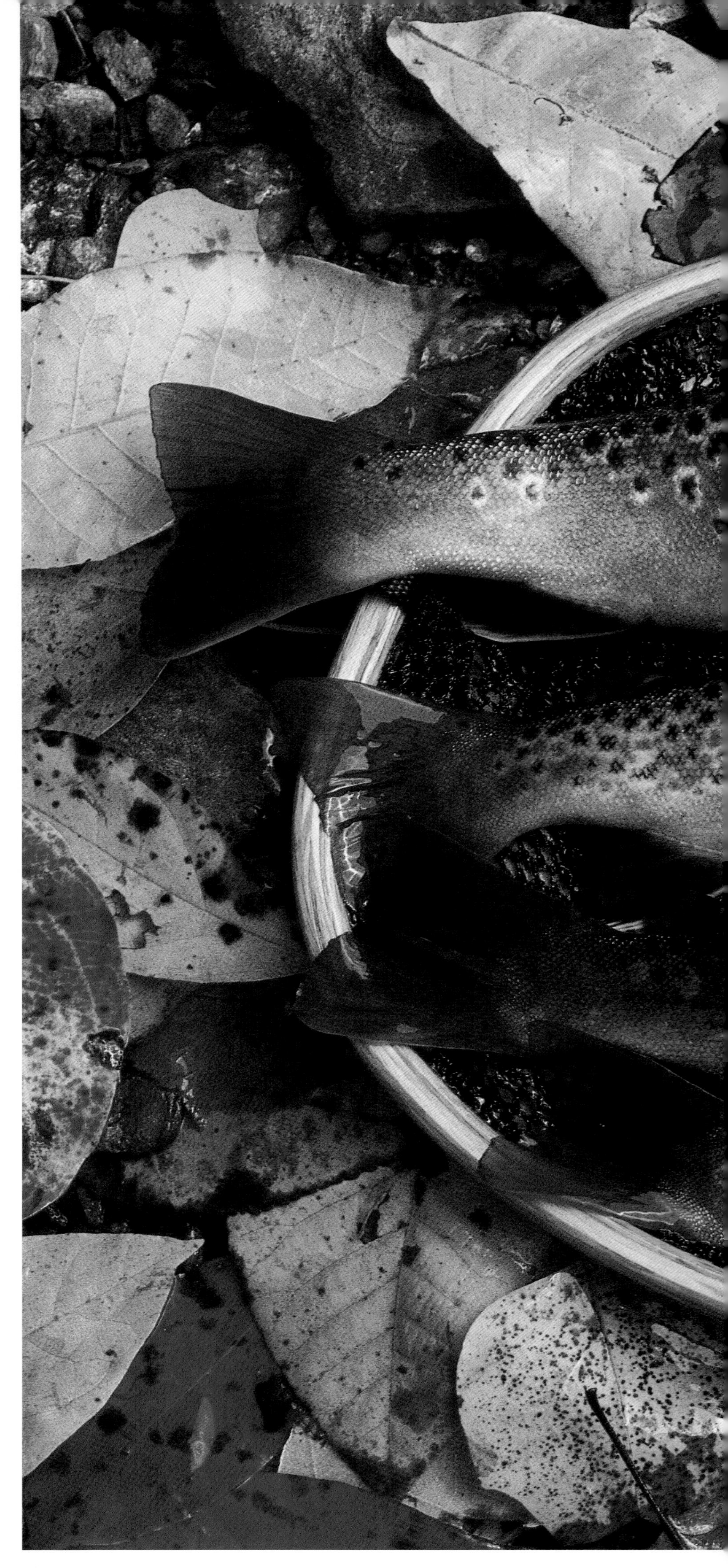

A lazy autumn afternoon along the Gunpowder River is a delightful escape from the modern world. Located in northern Baltimore County, this scenic waterway offers some of the Mid-Atlantic's best trout fishing, a fact known to many a fly fisherman **(above)**. *The key to such a successful fishery is a constant minimum flow of cold water released from the depths of Prettyboy Dam, and a heavily shaded river valley; trout cannot survive in warm water. The Department of Natural Resources regularly releases hatchery-raised rainbow and brown trout* **(right)**, *which are successfully spawning in the river along with a handful of native brook trout.*

Following pages: *No fear of heights for this skilled rock climber, ascending a jagged tower nicknamed "Strawberry Jam" at Rocks State Park in Harford County. Other popular rock climbing sites in the state include the Maryland Heights and Annapolis Rocks, both located along the Appalachian Trail.*

32710
73353
Yellow Jacket
CRESCENDO

Windswept on the Chesapeake Bay, sailboats of many varieties may be seen cruising its hundreds of square miles of navigable waters. A passenger takes the helm of Pride of Baltimore II **(above)**, *an authentic replica of the renowned Baltimore clippers of the 1800s. Licensed to carry passengers, the 157-foot ship sails as an ambassador for Maryland, visiting ports across the globe to promote economic development and tourism. Yachts* **(left)** *race nose-to-nose off Annapolis, sailing capital of the East, where many a competitive sailor has found paradise. The fun-loving crew of a log canoe* **(below)** *rides the boards to prevent capsizing. Vintage workboats of yesteryear adapted for sailing, the unique log canoe only numbers about twenty remaining vessels, many of which race along the Miles River near St. Michael's.*

Maryland's oldest equestrian sport is alive and well across our winter landscape. Contrary to popular belief, the purpose of the hunt is not to kill its wily quarry, but to provide a vigorous chase for the club's members **(left)**. *Jumps are scattered over most foxhunting territories to add excitement for the riders, and the hounds also relish the challenge* **(below)**. *The flashy red jackets, called "dress pinks," are worn only by the hunt's officers and staff, including a huntsman* **(right)** *who gives commands to the hounds, both verbally and by horn. The foxhunting season in Maryland runs from September to March.*

Above and below: *One of the toughest jobs in Maryland is oystering along the Chesapeake Bay during the winter months, whether hand-tonging or dredging by the celebrated skipjacks, the last remaining commercial fishing vessels in North America to use sail power. Annual harvests today are a mere fraction of oystering's heyday in the late 1800s; the culprits are over-harvesting, pollution, and the spread of parasitic diseases MSX and Dermo, which, though harmless to humans, wreak havoc on young oysters. This bivalve is a critical component of the Chesapeake ecosystem, for it cleanses the bay's water by filtering minute particles of food. The nooks and crannies of oyster bars also create habitat for an assortment of marine animals.*

Left: *A lobster pot is hauled from the Atlantic Ocean sixty miles off Maryland's coastline. One hundred fathoms below, lobsters hide in crevices by day and feed at night, crushing their prey with the larger foreclaw and shredding the flesh with the smaller claw, combed with fine teeth. Lobsters are well-known for their longevity; this two-foot giant in the left box may very well have been a youngster when the S.S.* Titanic *sank after striking an iceberg in 1912.*

Above and following pages: *Churning whitewater lures spectators and world-class kayakers to the Savage River in Garrett County, home to the World Whitewater Canoe/Kayak Championships in 1989 and Olympic Trials in 1992. During the 1989 event, 300 athletes representing twenty-five countries entertained crowds upwards of 20,000 during the first world championships hosted in America.*

Right: *Concluding a break from the challenging "Upper Yough" whitewater, rafters engage the river once again. This eleven-mile odyssey on the Upper Youghiogheny River in western Garrett County passes through a remote wilderness river canyon, boasting some twenty major rapids and spectacular natural scenery. Along the middle canyon, the river drops an average of 116 feet per mile, creating a wild ride.*

dib

Deep-sea fishermen with Captain Ben Gilbreath (holding tuna, below) usually have their hands full. When a school of dolphin is encountered, a score or more may be fished from the deep-blue waters with fly rods during feeding frenzies. Fresh from the ocean, dolphinfish **(left)** *are "lit-up," glowing with beautiful hues of yellow, green, and blue, but the brilliant colors often fade within seconds. Yellowfin tuna* **(below)** *are also prized by fishermen, for they put up a good fight, and, at an average of fifty pounds, each fish contains plenty of fillets. The most coveted fish of all is the white marlin* **(above)**. *The "king of gamefish," a prolific jumper, is very finicky and great skill is required to hook and land him. This fish, like the vast majority of marlins caught today, was released after being photographed.*

Harvesting wildlife is a deep-rooted tradition that challenges the skills of some 150,000 Marylanders annually. Bow-hunting for whitetails (left) *and gunning for geese* (above) *are especially popular. Other targeted animals include the turkey, squirrel, rabbit, duck, dove, and quail. Commonly trapped furbearers in Maryland include the muskrat, beaver, red fox, and raccoon. Though objectionable to some people, these activities offer an intimate connection to the natural world that casual observation of wildlife often cannot. Revenues generated by hunting and trapping are important to the local economy and help to finance the state's Wildlife and Heritage Division, which sets bag limits as a wildlife management tool to curb the population of many animals to a healthy level.*

Once a sleepy little community in Maryland's hinterland, Deep Creek Lake is now a year-round destination. In addition to boating, water-skiing, swimming, and fishing at the lake, nearby attractions offer skiing, snowboarding, hiking, camping, and whitewater rafting. The lake was formed in 1925 when Deep Creek was dammed to generate electricity. Though it is only twelve miles long, its many fingers create about sixty-five miles of shoreline. On peak summer weekends, the population may swell by several thousand, but it rarely seems congested; peace and quiet are easily found.

Above: *A scenic section of Little Falls, which feeds into the Gunpowder River, is an inviting stop along the Northern Central Railroad Trail, a twenty-mile hiker-biker corridor that runs from Cockeysville north to Pennsylvania. The rails and wooden ties have been replaced by crushed stone, accommodating a smooth trip for bicyclists and pedestrians by the thousands. Beside its convenience, with nine access points, the Northern Central Railroad Trail is extremely popular for its bounty of natural scenery, everything from beavers to beech trees, ferns to frogs, and brook trout to bloodroot flowers.*

Right: *The summit of Sugarloaf Mountain rises some 700 feet above the surrounding countryside in southern Frederick County. Sugarloaf is a classic monadnock, or isolated mountain, located in the Piedmont province several miles east of the Blue Ridge Mountains. Though privately owned, this National Natural Landmark is open to the public year-round. Scenic hiking trails, overlooks, and boulder piles which rise to the summit make Sugarloaf an ideal nature retreat. Early summer is a good time to visit, when the pinks and whites of blooming mountain laurel add splendor to the forest floor.*

Following pages: *Soaring in the domain of hawks, which often tag along, a hang glider enjoys the rustic scenery of Allegany County. This adventure sport has a small following in Maryland, largely due to a shortage of convenient launch sites. One notable exception is High Rock, located just off the Appalachian Trail near Pen Mar in Washington County.*

Above: *For those few willing to rise before 6 a.m. to catch the summer sun rising over the Atlantic Ocean, the experience is one of solitude, reflection, and replenishment. The gorgeous reds, yellows, and oranges that light up the skies at dawn and dusk are a result of these colors' longer wavelengths. The sun is then low to the horizon, and its light must pass through more atmosphere, allowing particles in the air to scatter and thus minimize colors with shorter wavelengths, such as blues and greens.*

Right: *A favorite haunt of Maryland paddlers is Mataponi Creek, which flows into the Patuxent River at Jug Bay. Here nature buffs can view a robust population of wild rice, at its best in mid-summer, when crowned by feathery flower spikes. Access is gained from a nearby boat launch at Patuxent River Park in Prince George's County.*

MARYLAND DNR
Wildlife Division

Thanks to helping hands from the Department of Natural Resources, some 500 species of native animals stand a better chance of survival. The bog turtle **(above)** *is one of North America's rarest turtles, and the northern reaches of central Maryland represent one of the species' last strongholds, a tenuous one at that. Due to poaching for the pet trade and degradation of its wetland habitat, this shy and elusive turtle is being considered for protection through endangered species status. Captured on the Eastern Shore, this river otter* **(left)** *is destined for a new life in western Maryland. Earlier this century, poor water quality, due to pollution generated by mining and logging, doomed the rambunctious otter in its mountain homeland, but recent improvements provide hope for a comeback.*

WESTERN MARYLAND
734

Travelers take in Maryland's natural scenery the old-fashioned way. On the first Sunday in May, the public is invited to walk across the bay via the 4.3 mile Chesapeake Bay Bridge (below). *From May to December passengers aboard the 1916 steam locomotive* Mountain Thunder (left) *are treated to extraordinary landscapes by the Western Maryland Scenic Railroad. A vintage carriage* (right) *rambles along the Northern Central Railroad Trail.*

Following pages: *The beaches of Ocean City frequently change their mood… at midday on peak summer weekends, the sand becomes prime real estate, playground for a quarter-million visitors. By late afternoon a sense of calm and peacefulness sweeps the shoreline.*

THE
MIRAGE

BUFFET

Above: *Gateway to western Maryland, the National Freeway (I-68) cuts through Sidling Hill just west of Hancock in Washington County. To the trained eye, the cross-sections in the exposed rock tell a vivid story of geologic upheaval in the earth's ever-changing crust, and the unusual shape of the folded rock layers has drawn national attention to this site. Hence a visitor's center and viewing platform were completed recently not only to provide a break for weary motorists, but also to educate people on the mountain's natural history.*

Right: *For those who are not quite ready for the rigors of cliff climbing, navigating across huge boulder piles is the next best thing. On many of Maryland's mountainsides, there are interesting outcrops where the vegetation and soil has eroded over the eons, exposing the underlying bedrock. Gravity exploits weak fissures in the rocks, and large chunks break off. Rocks can be slippery, and a long leap such as this maverick's is not recommended.*

Following pages: *Golfers at Pine Ridge Golf Course near Loch Raven in Baltimore County must not only contend with bunkers, water traps and trees, but also with squadrons of chunky, mobile lawnmowers which intercept many a golf ball. Resident Canada geese have taken a liking to area golf courses, where there is plenty of food, peace, and quiet—much to the dismay of weary groundskeepers.*

MD 130 AJ

Commercial and recreational fishermen haul in their catch, the striped bass, known locally as the rockfish. Fortunately, its delicious pearly meat can still be savored by Marylanders, but this celebrated Chesapeake fishery was recently pushed to the brink. From the early 1970s to the mid-1980s the harvests of both watermen and biologists, conducting annual surveys since 1954, recorded a rapid decline that necessitated immediate action; a ban was declared in 1985 to allow the remaining fish a chance to repopulate. Within five years the census data was encouraging, making a strong case for over-fishing as the chief stress. A limited season on stripers has since been reopened, but it is carefully monitored to avoid repeating mistakes of the past.

Since birds are relatively easy to find, abundant in many different types of habitat, and so diverse, birding has really taken off in recent years as Americans are becoming increasingly aware and appreciative of their natural heritage. This love affair with birds takes on a variety of forms. Birdwatching (left), *photography* (below), *feeding, landscaping, and, for a few dedicated enthusiasts, bird-banding, are collectively the nation's second most popular leisure time activity (gardening is first). Some of the beauties captured at the Irvine Natural Science Center's banding station include* (above, left to right) *the indigo bunting, downy woodpecker, and Canada warbler. Over time, the information recorded by banders helps scientists identify trends and problems, to which conservationists can then respond.*

5

Above: *Swimmers at Cascade Lake take flight from the high-jump platform. This old-time summertime park is tucked away in the picturesque countryside of northern Carroll County near Snydersburg. Like Cascade, all of Maryland's lakes and ponds are man-made.*

Left: *Taking adventure to the extreme, a kayaker runs "The Spout," a twenty-two-foot chute at Great Falls which only the most experienced kayakers dare to challenge. This stretch of the Potomac, where the river drops some seventy-six feet in less than a mile, creates a paddler's paradise, with waterfalls, rapids, and rugged natural scenery. On all but the coldest of weekends, scores of whitewater enthusiasts, called "river runners," can be seen from various perches on the cliffs. The best viewing occurs on the Virginia side.*

There's no better way to enjoy a sunset than with a baited hook, waiting for dinner to strike. At the Ocean City Inlet (below) *an angler reels in a small fish, but there will be plenty more, as strong currents supply a steady flow of "keepers." At Sandy Point State Park* (right), *framed by the Bay Bridge, a fisherman waits for a nibble, hopefully that of an adult striped bass, which at a typical weight of ten to twenty pounds, will put up a good fight. Surf fishing* (bottom right) *along the Atlantic beaches can be hit or miss, depending on tides, location of sandbars, weather, and other variables. The unpredictability also applies to the catch— will it be a shark, skate, bluefish, sea trout, kingfish or flounder?*

Acknowledgments

A Special Thanks to…

My unofficial support team—Dave Brinker, Brent Trautman, Dick Wiegand, Bob Rinker, Gerda Deterer, Robert Colona, Scott Smith, Tom Dembeck, Dee Thompson, Nick Spero, Kevin Dodge, Joe Ondek, and Joan Maloof… without your gift of time, experience, and energy, many of these photographs would not have been possible

My parents, Bob and Shiny Evans, for their continued dedication to the success of Middleton Press

Betsy Hughes, for her unabated enthusiasm and thoughtful editing of *Maryland's Great Outdoors*

Judie Deakins and Lynn Gurtler, for helping to prepare the copy for editing

Elizabeth Roman, of Baseline Graphics, for her diligent formatting of this book for printing

Jack Warns and Fanilya Gueno, of True Color Professional Lab, for printing the layout proofs

Rhonda Hughes and Samantha Soma, of Print Vision, for their expertise in coordinating the overseas printing.

Glenn Therres, of the Maryland Department of Natural Resources, for approving my most ambitious project

I would also like to recognize those individuals who lent a much appreciated helping hand:

Bill Barber
Andrew Barclay
Fraser Bishop
James Bond
Paul Brinsfield
Phil Coleman
Richard Cook
Keith Costley
Lauren Costley
Gene Deems
Phoebe DeVoe
Kirk Dreier
Sue Ellenberg
Joe Ennis
Dan Feller
Logan Fitzhugh
Bonnie Friend
Jim Forrester
Doug Gary
Ben Gilbreath
Charlie Gougeon
Mary Groves
Kenneth Hall
Keith Harrison
Pat Hawes
Tim Hoen
Heidi Hughes
Janice Hughlett
Robert Joiner
Margot Lambros
Dana Limpert
Peter Martin
Steve McDaniel
Denise McNamara
Chuck Motsko
Corrine Parks
Wendy Paskus
Will Rambo
Barbara Ross
Greg Rouse
Jim Rowan
Rick Maloof
Tom Mathews
Arnold Norden
Doug Sampson
Beverly Sauls
Marc Schenck
Edwin Smith
Bob Stanhope
Charles Stine
Bill Trautman
Bill Vanscoy
Donald Webster
Al Wesche
Doug Wigfield
Jean Worthley

Index

THOSE CURIOUS NEW CULTS

William J. Petersen has also written

ANOTHER HAND ON MINE

ASTROLOGY AND THE BIBLE

With Russell T. Hitt

SHARE YOUR FAITH

THOSE CURIOUS NEW CULTS

William J. Petersen

KEATS PUBLISHING, INC.  NEW CANAAN, CONNECTICUT

Those Curious New Cults

Published in 1973 by Keats Publishing, Inc.

212 Elm Street, New Canaan, Connecticut 06840

ISBN 87983-031-X

Library of Congress Catalog Card Number: 72-93700

Printed in the United States of America

Contents

Introduction

One spring afternoon in Amsterdam, as I was strolling near Dam Square with my family, we spotted some Hare Krishna devotees doing their thing across the street. Curious, my son Ken went over to get a closer look. These chanting, swaying religionists were young people from America too, and about Ken's age. Totally dedicated, they were willing to make fools of themselves for Krishna Consciousness. Apparently, they had finally found something to believe in.

Back home again in the States, I became increasingly fascinated by the hold that these new religions are having upon people today; and I also became increasingly concerned about Christian churches and parents whose examples had inspired youth to boredom and disdain. So I began writing a brief series of sketches on contemporary cults for *Eternity* Magazine, and thanks to Nathan Keats and Donald Kauffman this has blossomed into a book.

In the following pages I want you to get a closer look at Hare Krishna and fifteen other "curious new cults." You may wish that I had added a few more to the list or that my treatment of some of them would have been more exhaustive. But I am writing not for scholars but for young people and their parents who are looking for something to believe in.

This book I am dedicating to my son Ken, who has found Someone to believe in.